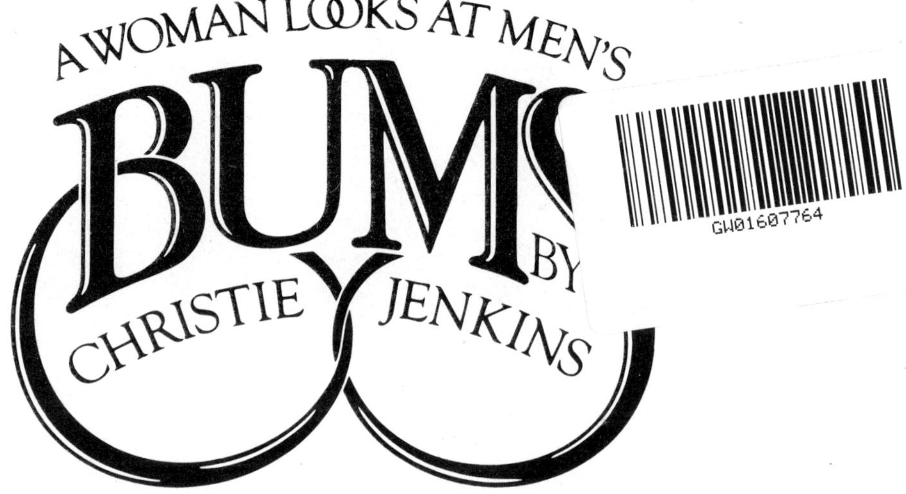

Christie Jenkins

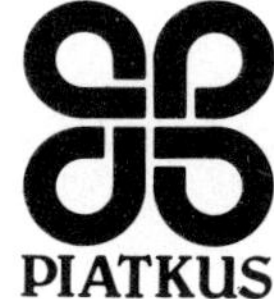

This book is dedicated to
BETTY AND PEPPER JENKINS,
who love and support me
in everything I do.

First published in Great Britain in 1983 by
Judy Piatkus (Publishers) Limited of Loughton Essex

ISBN 0 86188 247 4

Book design by Elizabeth Woll

Printed by The Garden City Press Ltd,
Letchworth, Herts

British Library Cataloguing in Publication Data

Jenkins, Christie
Bums: a woman looks at men's.
1. Photography of men
I. Title
779′.2′0924 TR654

Special thanks and acknowledgment to the following:

to TJ McCavitt for all you've been to me this year,
to Debbie Struble, Kevin Golden, Werner Erhard, and pterodactyl, for friendship, assistance, and space,
to John Herzfeld, actor/writer/director, for being on the cover,
to the people of The First Christian Church of North Hollywood, for your light and energy,
to Graphicolor, Simco, and particularly the people of ArtCraft Darkrooms for their fast and terrific service,
to Douglas Peter for the back cover photograph,
and to Peter de Bretteville and Sal Annino, for numerous things, including cameras and equipment.

Introduction

I remember seeing a hoarding when I was nine years old. On it, a little girl looked askance as a dog pulled off her bikini bottoms. The purpose was to show her tan line, but all I could think of was how embarrassing it would be to bare your behind in public.

Somewhere over the years, my attitude about the behind changed. It probably began at age seventeen with my total fascination with Rudolph Nureyev. By the time I was nineteen, my bedroom in Dallas was covered with his pictures, but my favourite pose was taken from the back. "What muscles," I would gush showing off my collection. "This is how God intended man to look." By age twenty-four and now in Los Angeles, I was saying, "Want to see a great ass?"

About three years ago, some girlfriends and I were sitting in an outdoor café. Suddenly, a great looking body passed by our table. We all turned in unison only to catch each other appreciating the rear view. What a laugh we had! It was the first time any of us knew we liked the same thing. Later I was teased into taking my first bum shots at a big tennis match that night. I had always loved sitting behind the serve line to watch Butch Walts, but this time my date got suspicious when I brought my camera and "snapped at all the wrong times." Butch laughed when I told him the story and asked him to be in this book. And he was pleased. Very pleased.

And that's been the reaction. Now, I am kidded about being a bum connoisseur. I can tell the athlete from the occasional jogger from the desk-prone executive. At parties, men ask for ratings as they shyly walk by. Coming or going, there's always something to smile at.

Once, I stopped two men on the street to ask them to be in this book. One said his wife would kill him and the other wanted to be paid. After that I stuck to men I knew or friends of friends—with the exception of a great looking guy I caught walking into my local Safeway. He, incidently, soon after became the love of my life.

This fun project has ended, so to speak. My girlfriends all envied me for what they considered a terrific opening line. Take a look at your guy's bum. If you see mostly keys and wallets, invest quickly in pocketless trousers. And enjoy what God hath created!

—Christie Jenkins

SOME FRIENDS

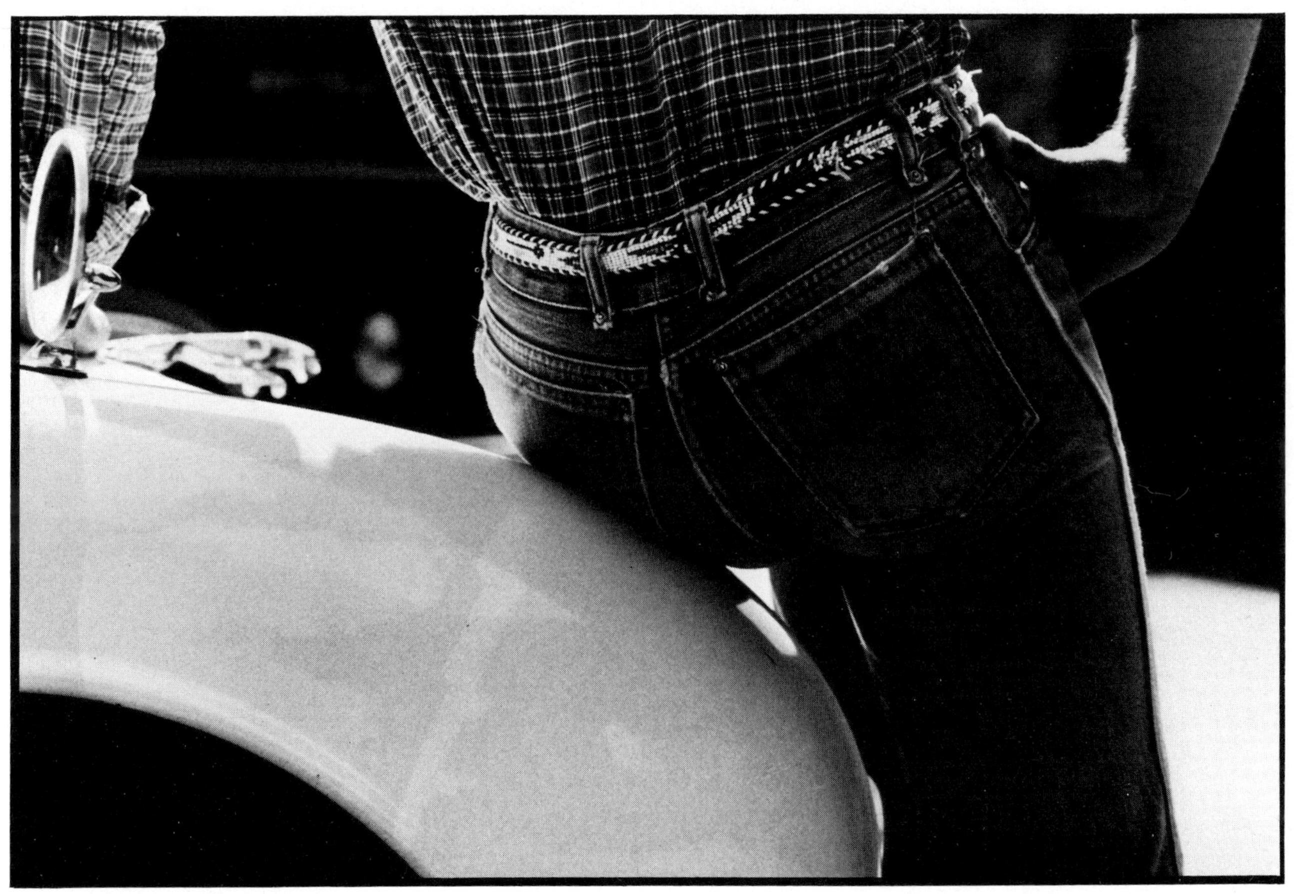

BRUCE

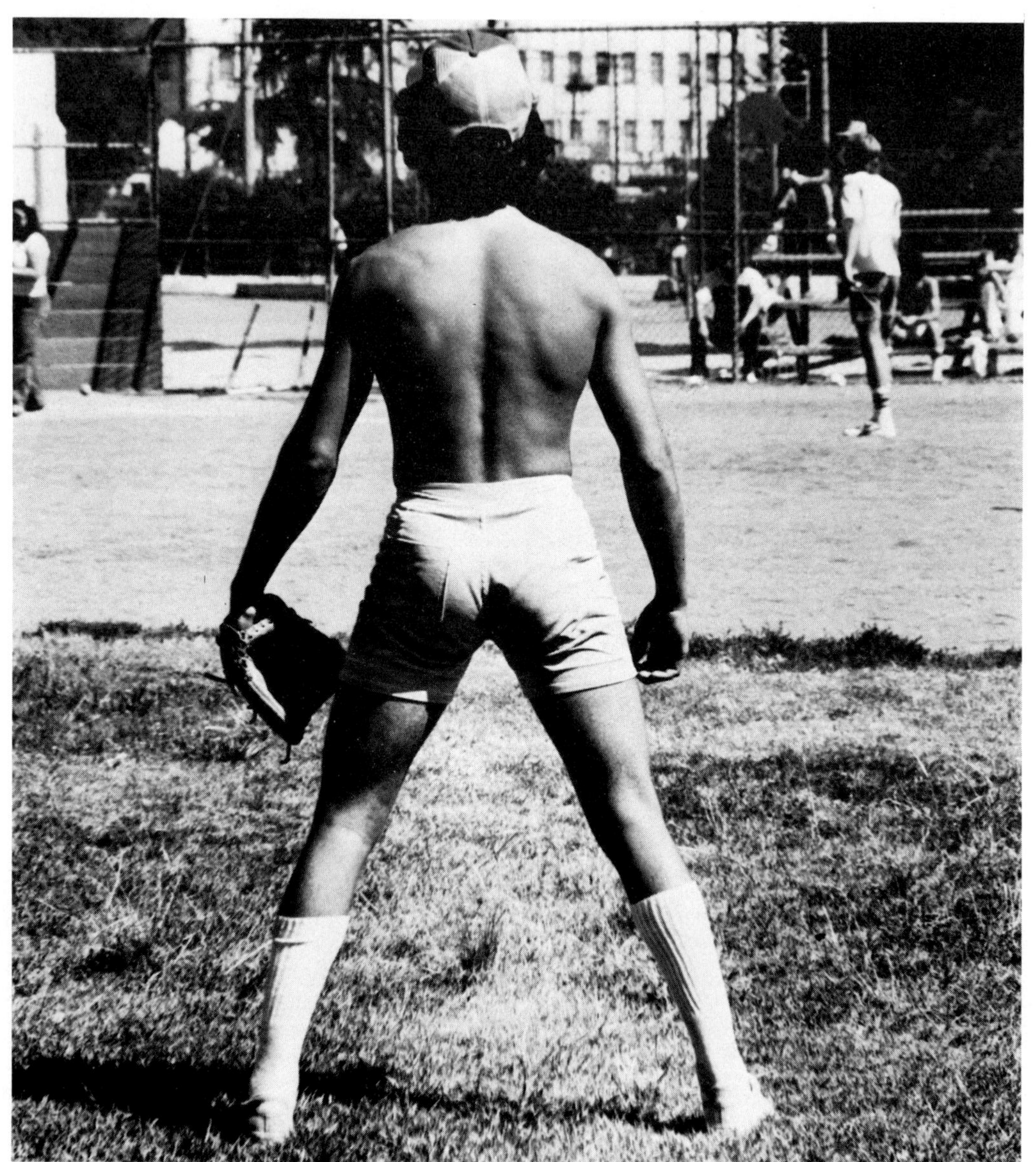

ROGER

MICKEY/musician

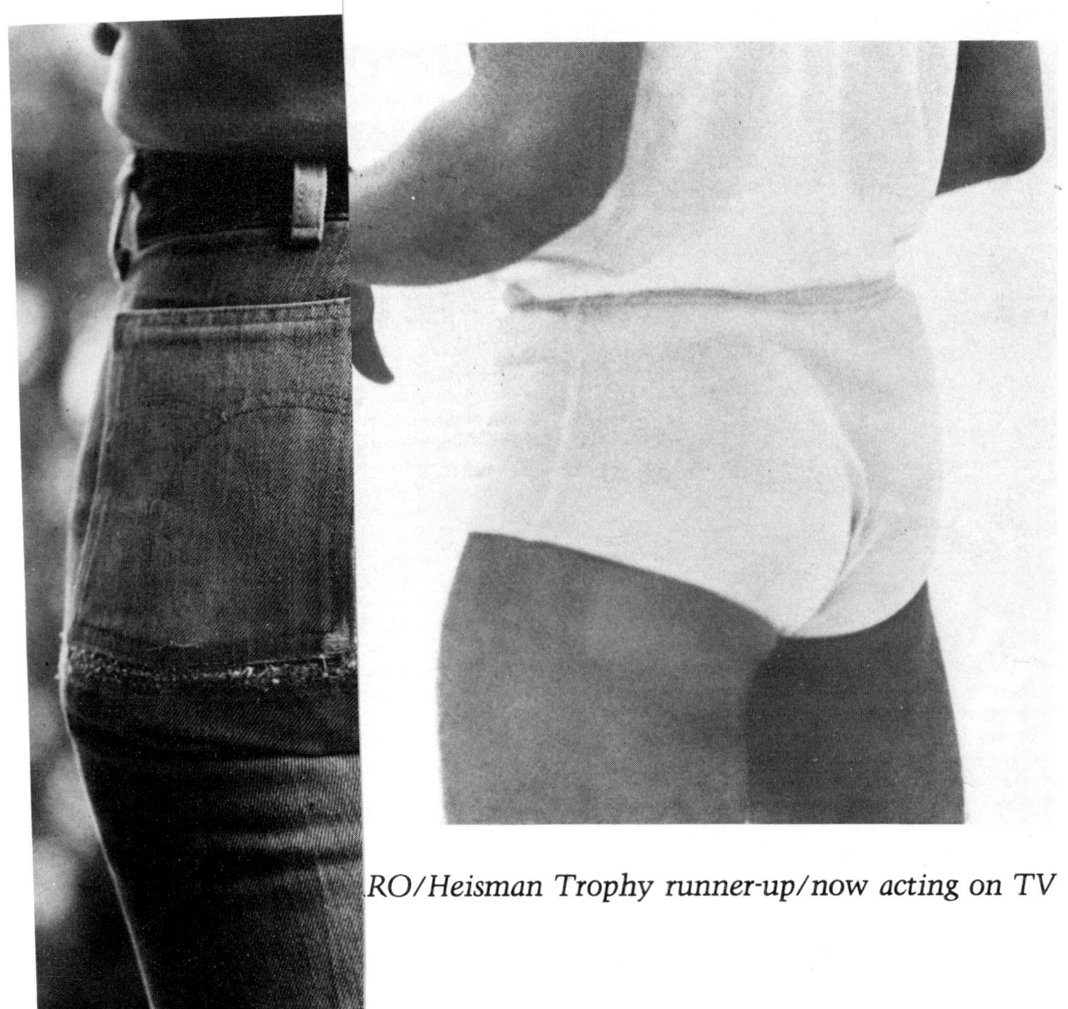

RO/Heisman Trophy runner-up/now acting on TV

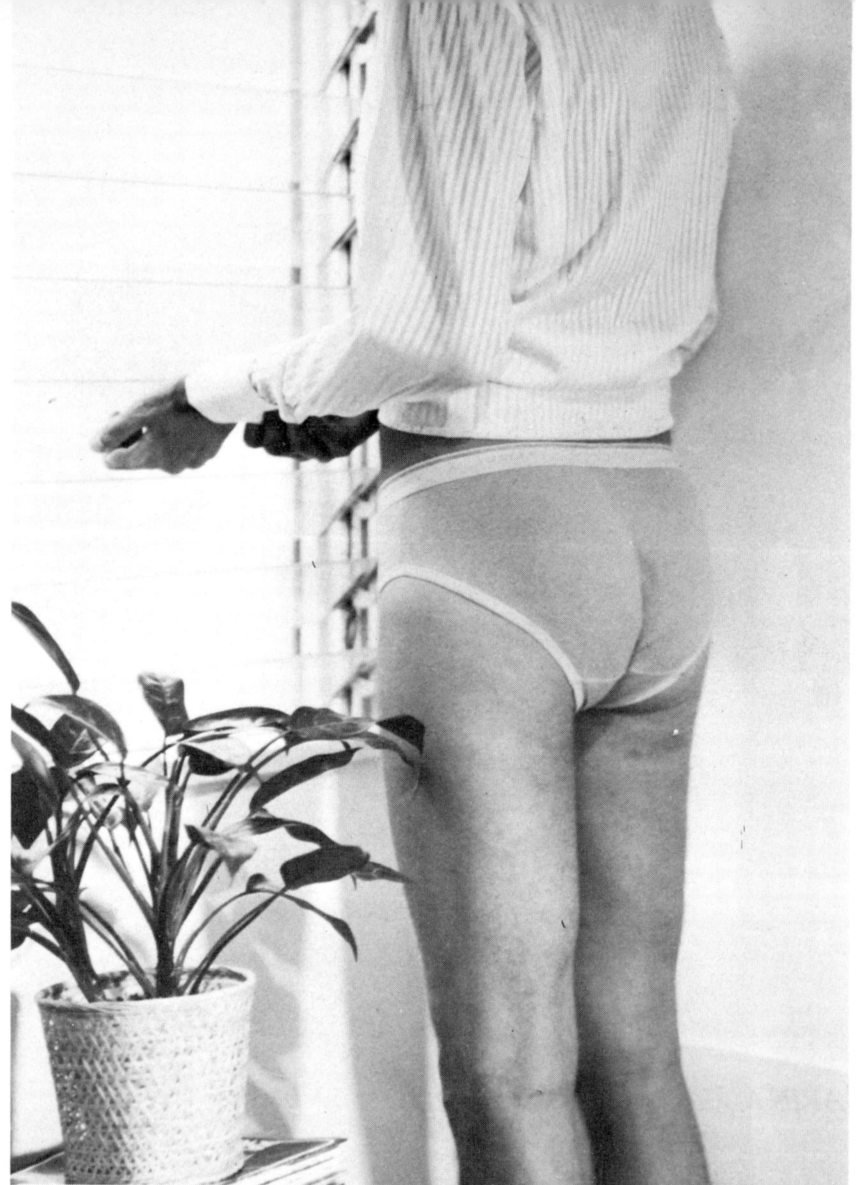

MICHAEL/drummer

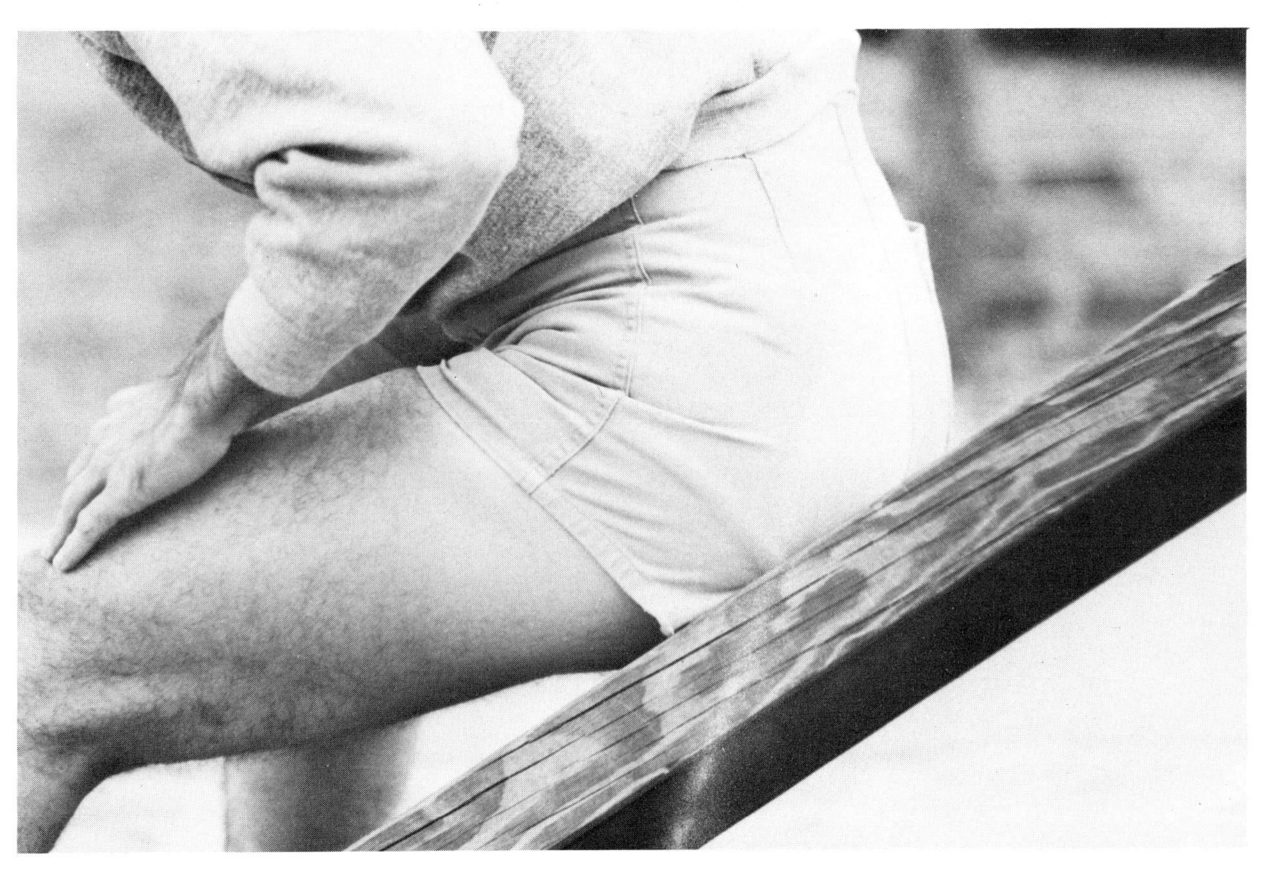

T. JAMES/model

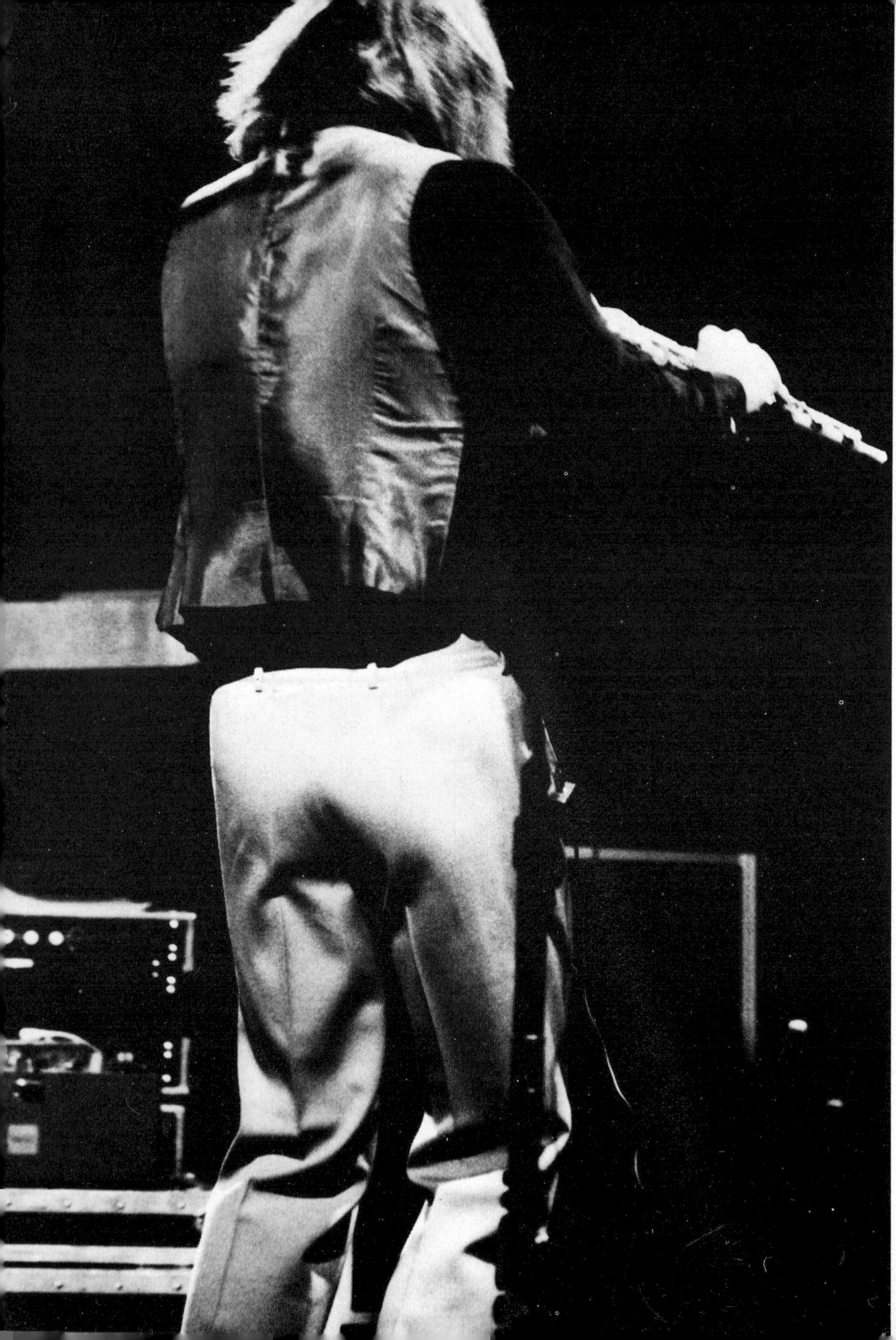

TIM WEISBERG/
flutist/composer/
recording artist

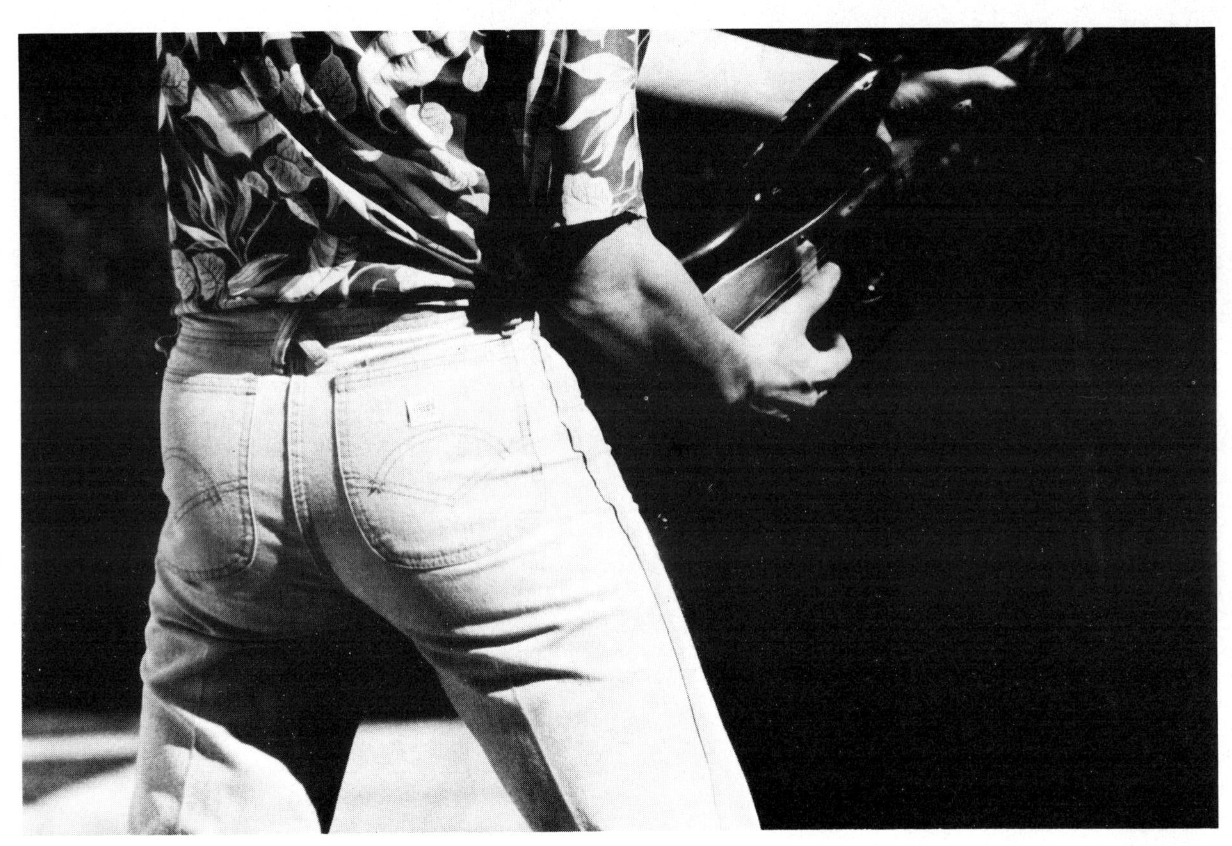

DAVID CASSIDY

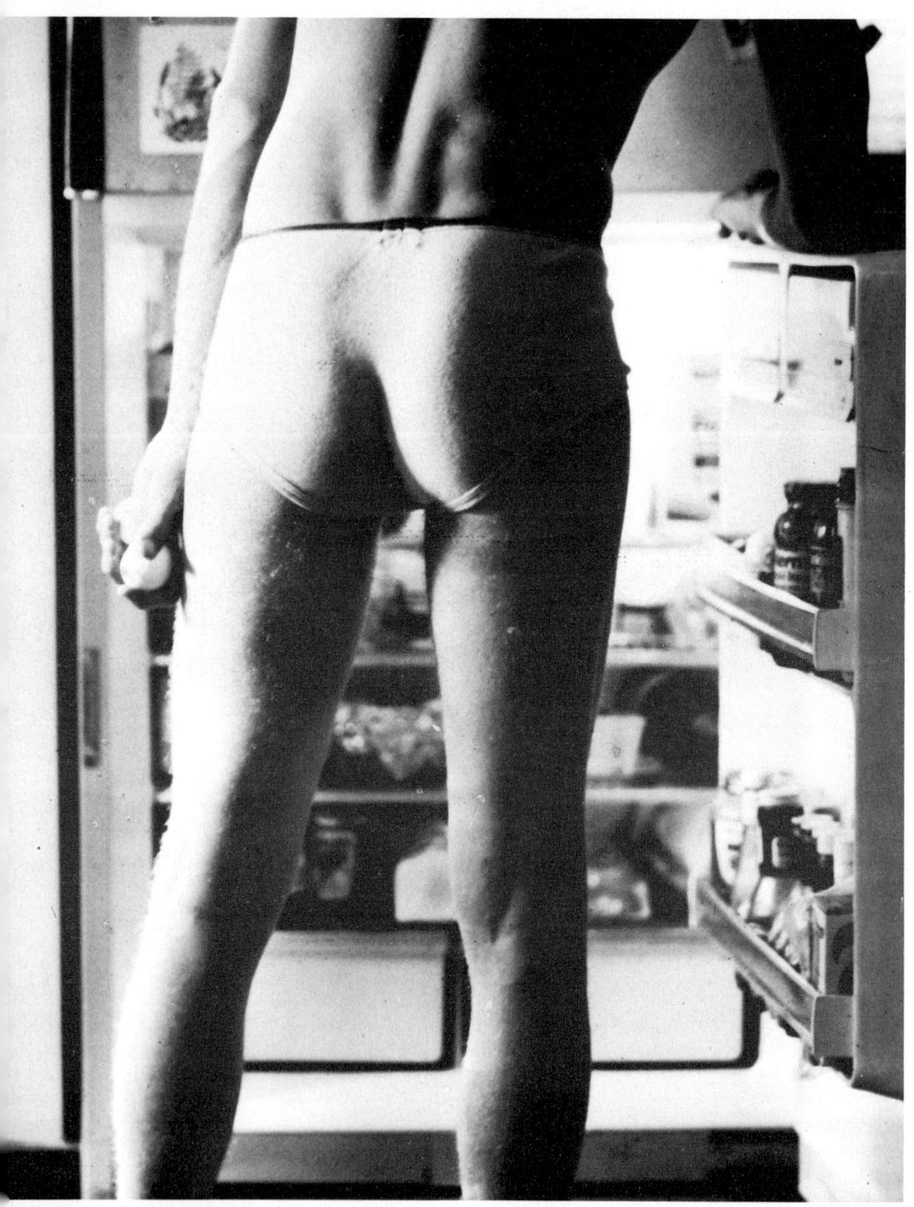

TERO

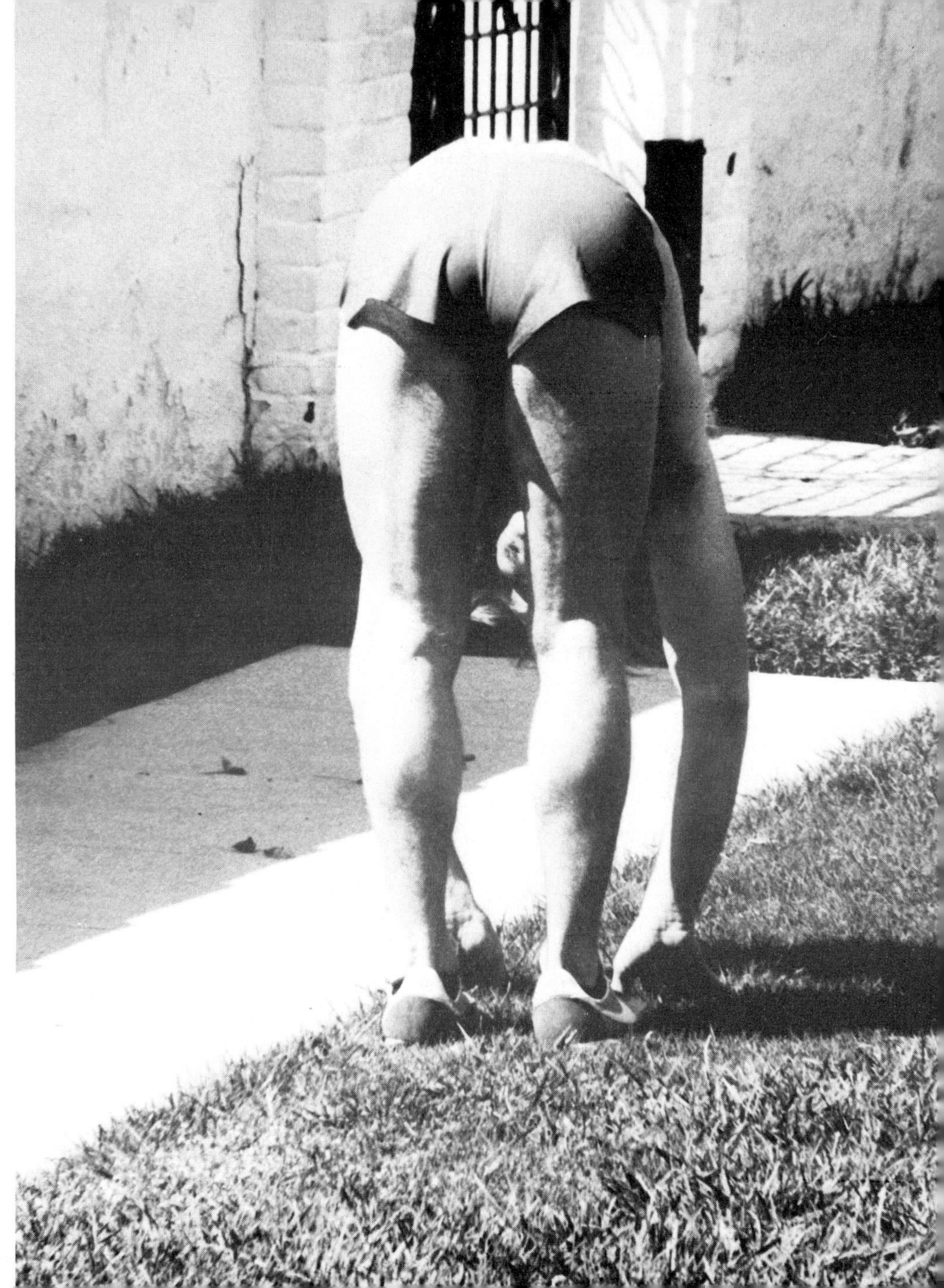

FLIP/sailor/healer

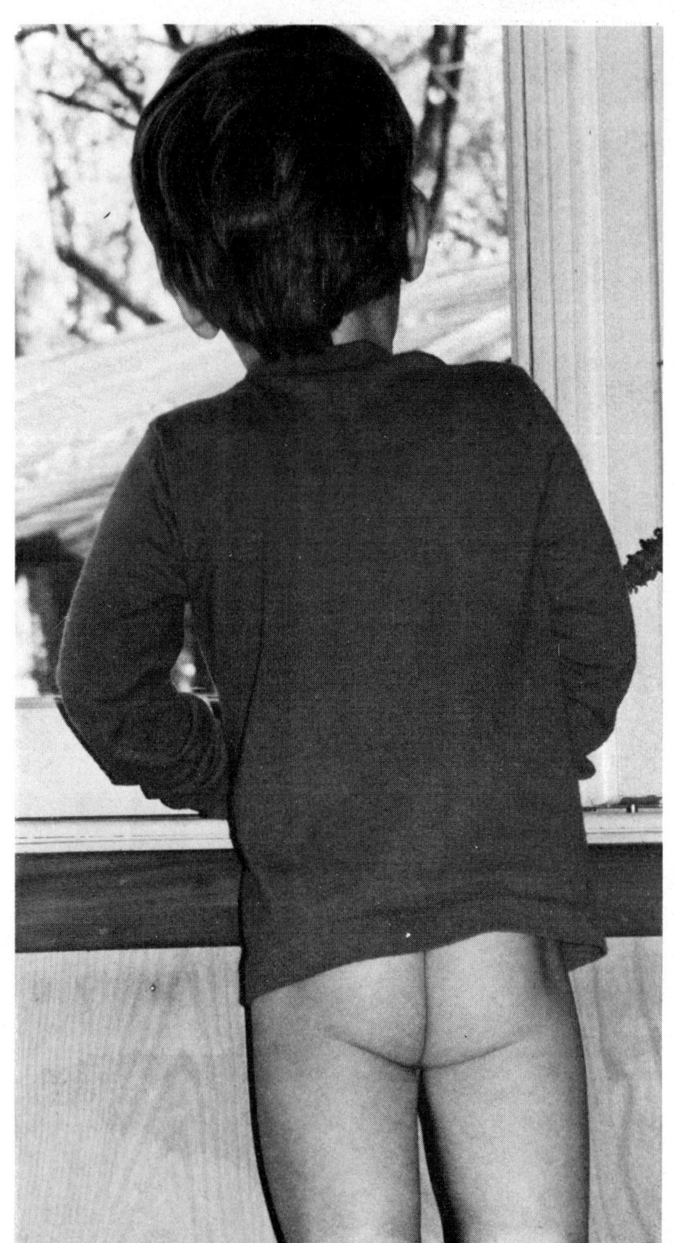

BABY BRENT

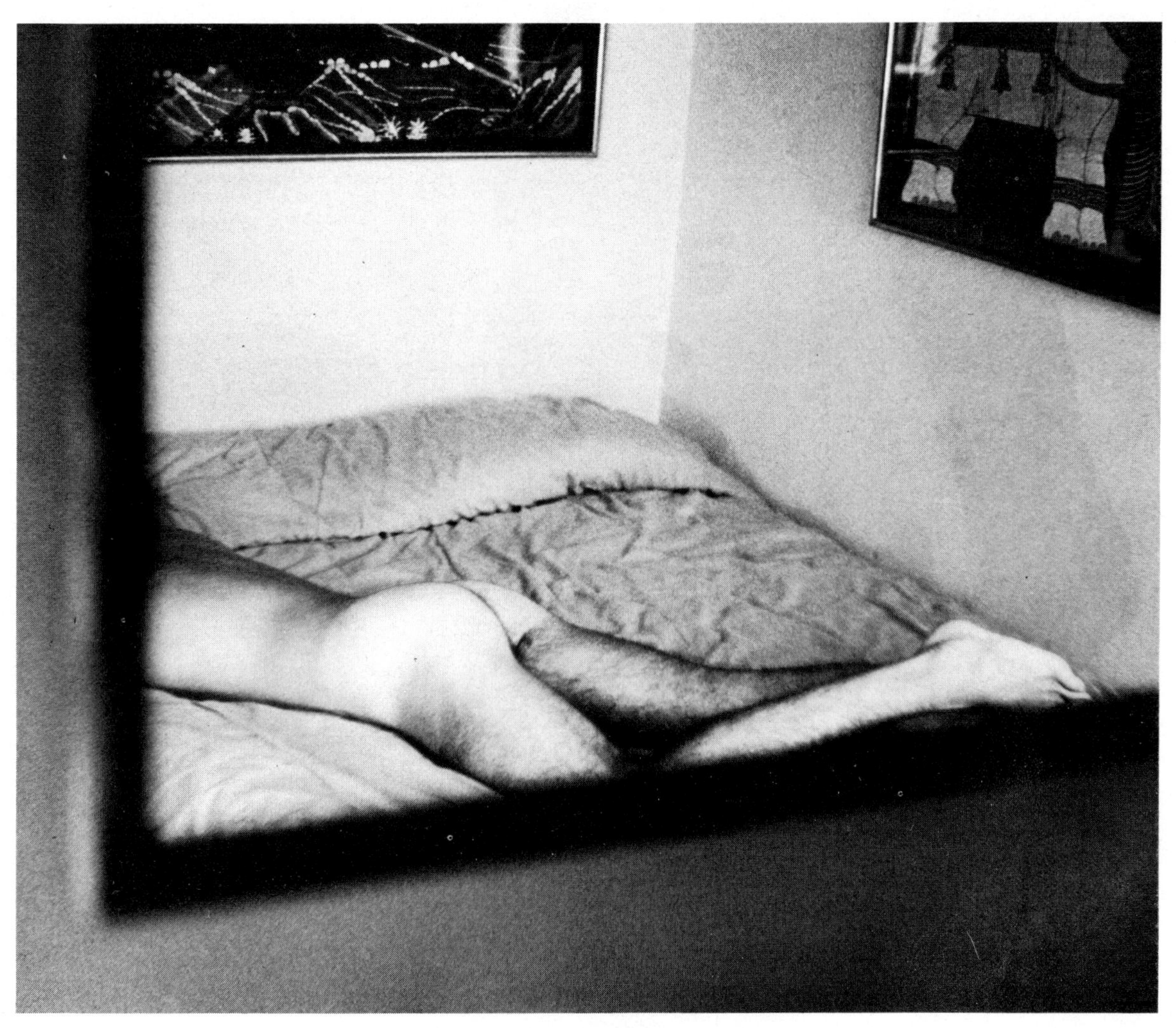

BIG BABY

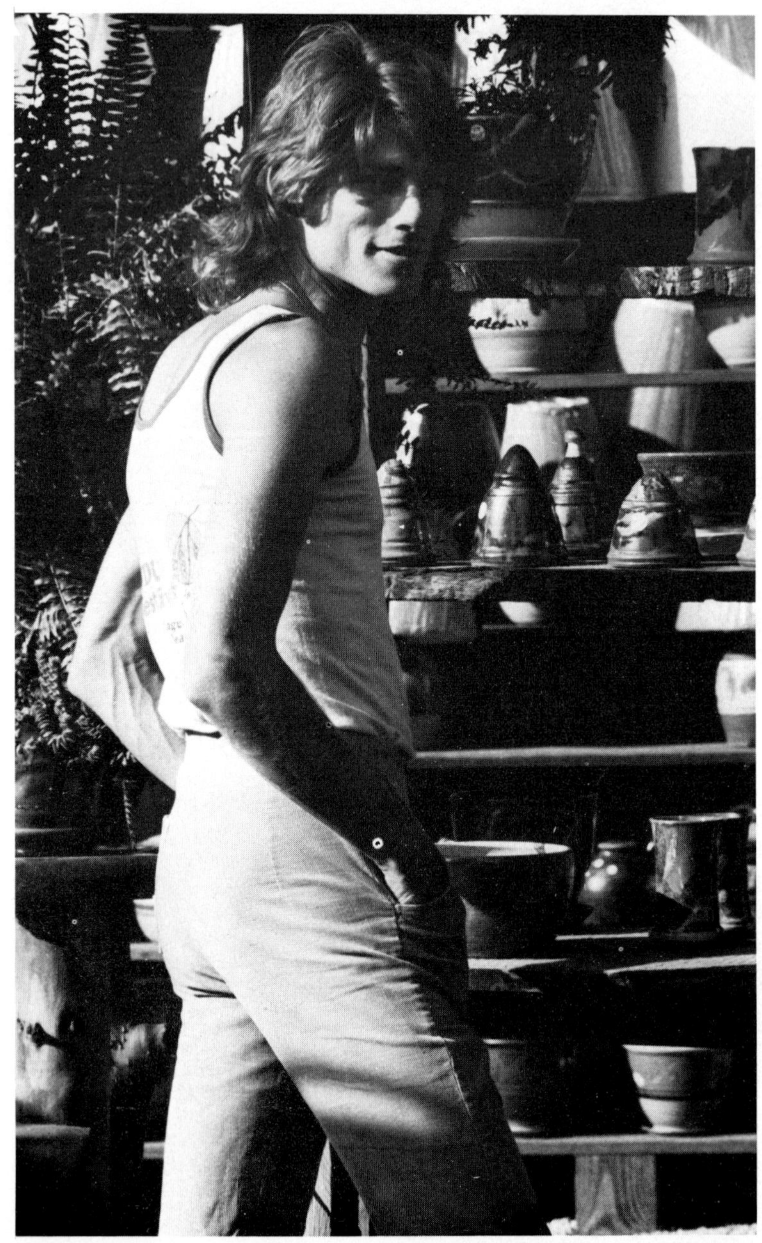

BILL/Laguna Beach potter

ROBBIE

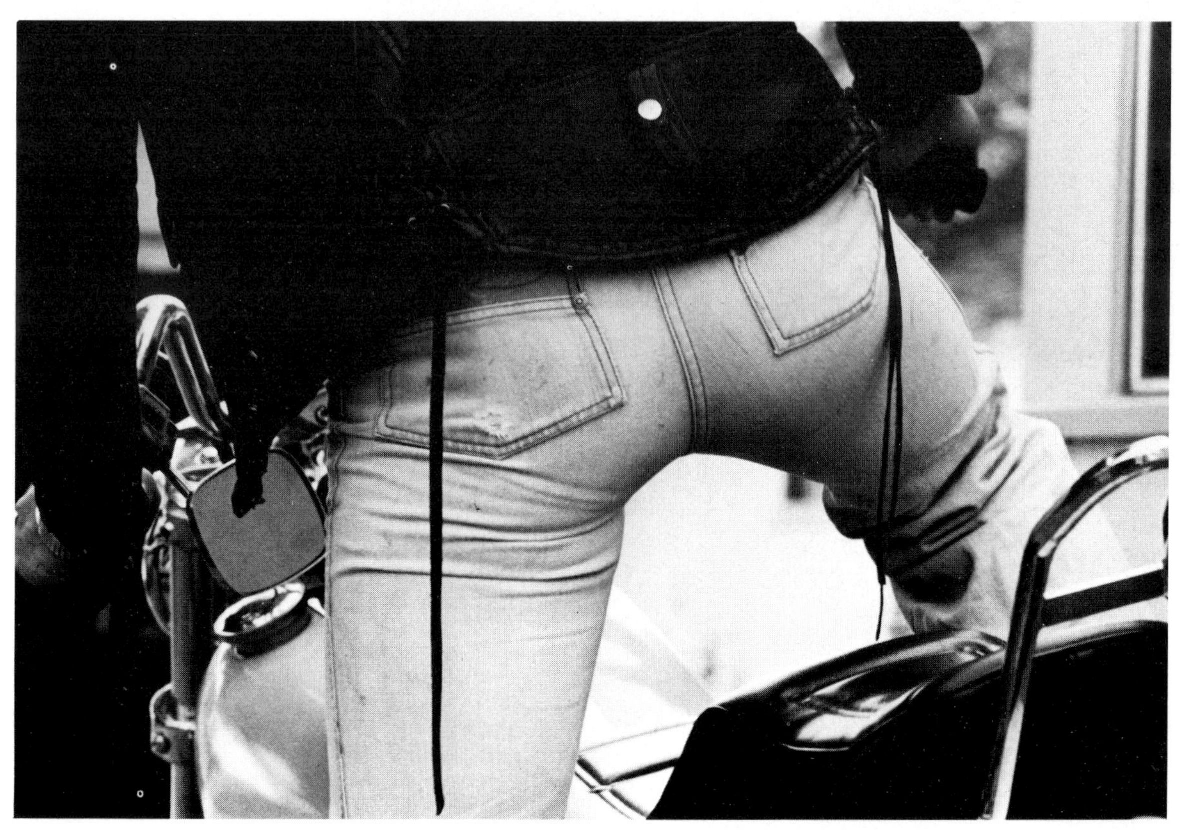

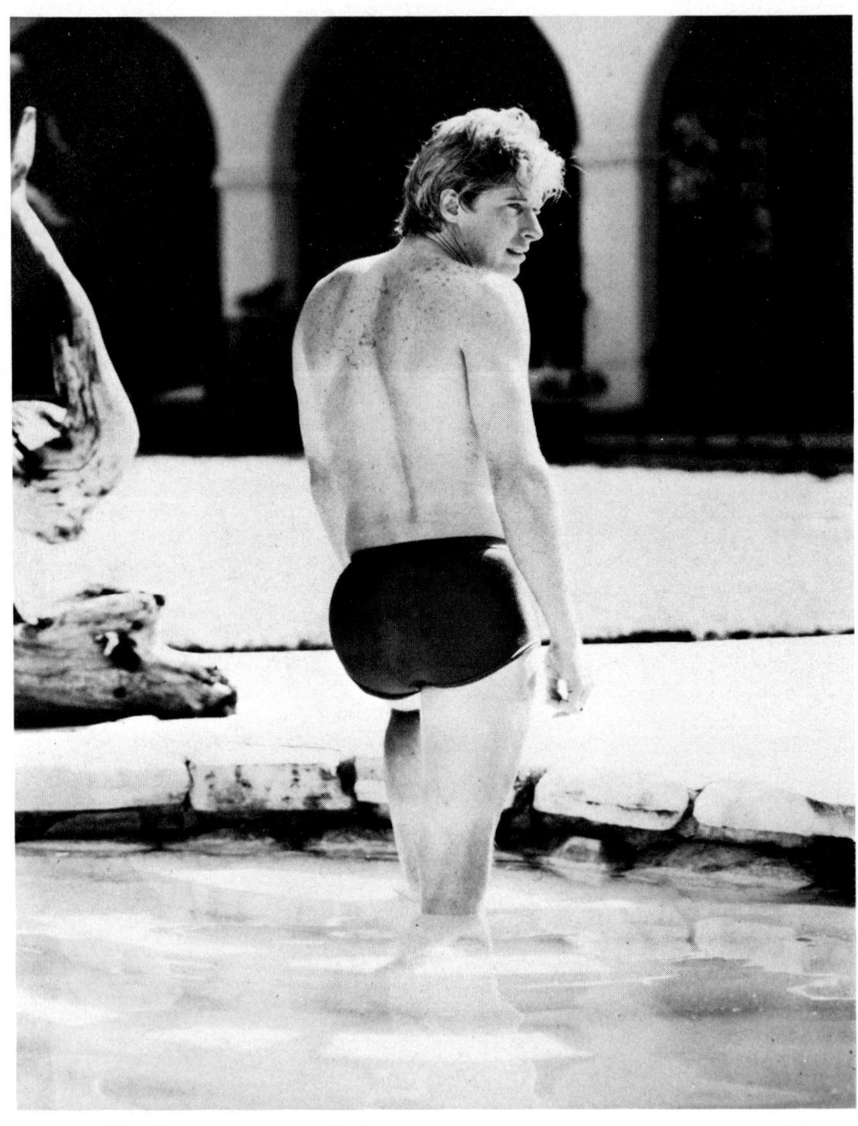

JOHN/actor-producer

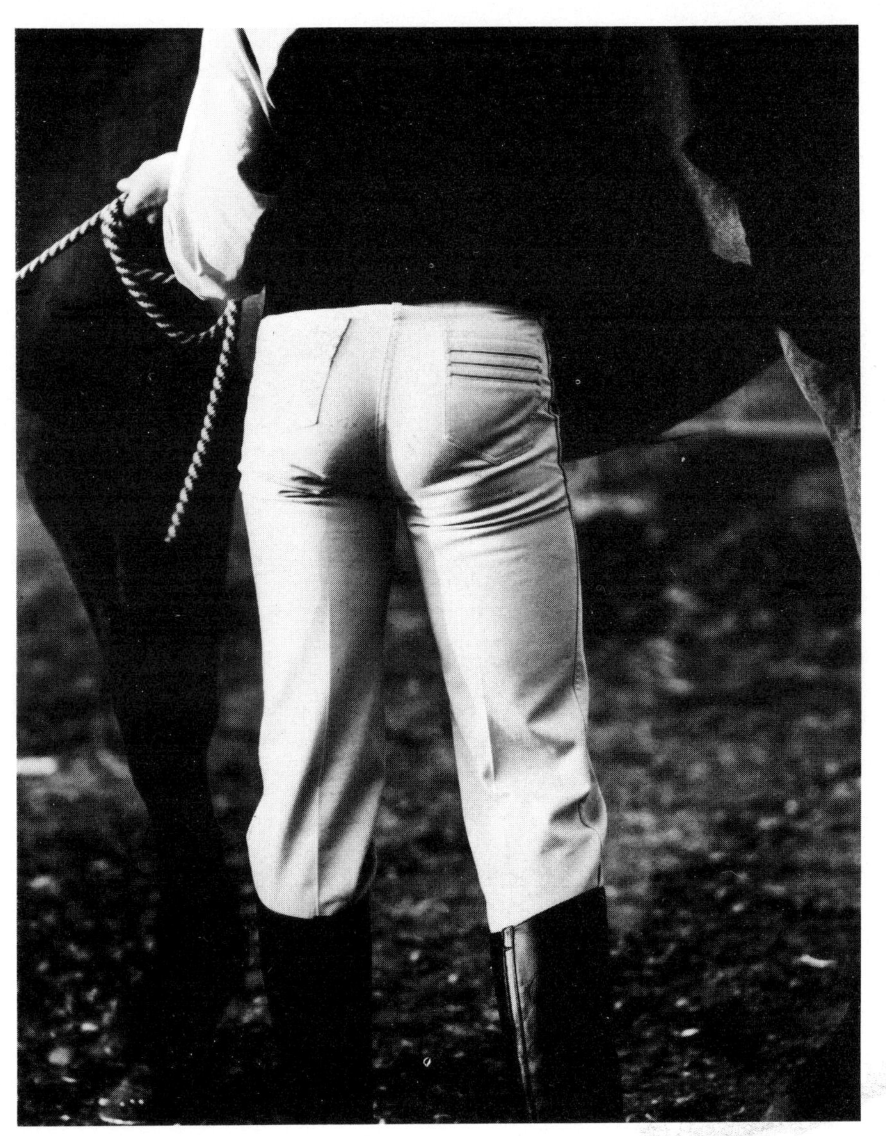

BARNEY

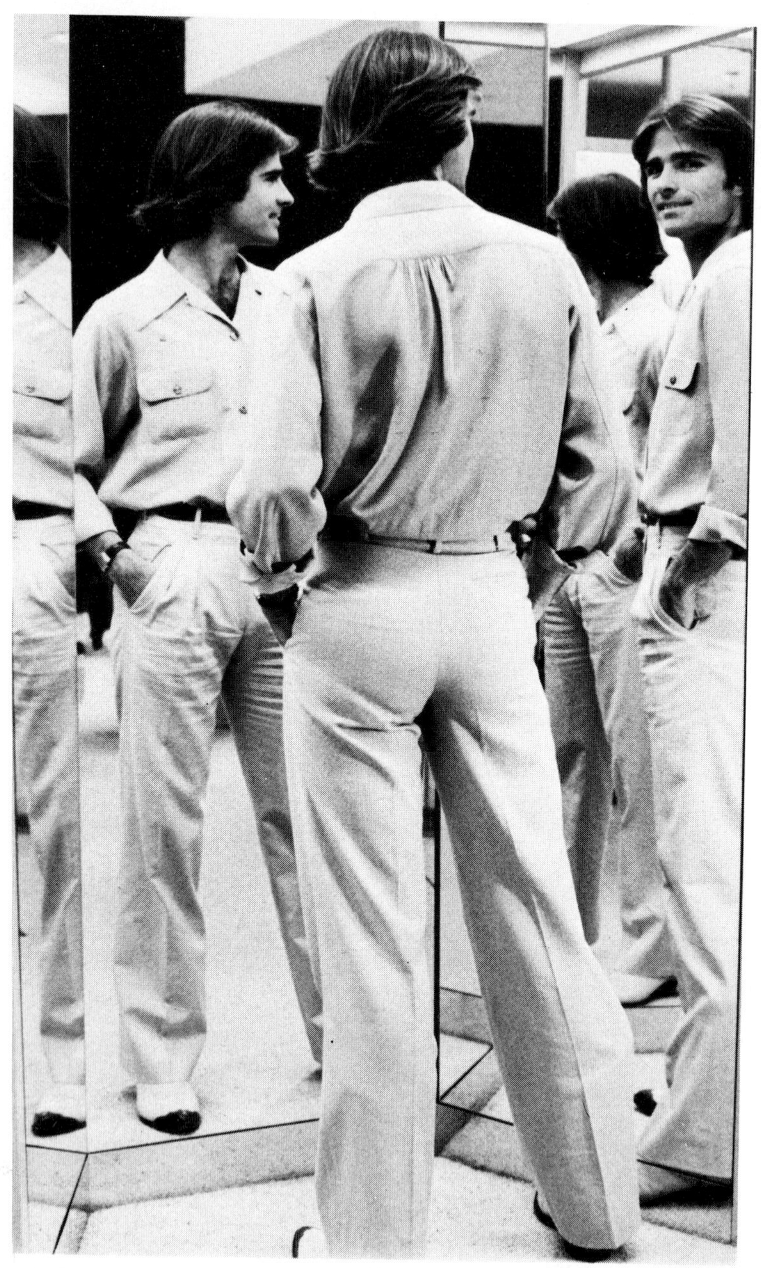

TJ/All American Heartthrob

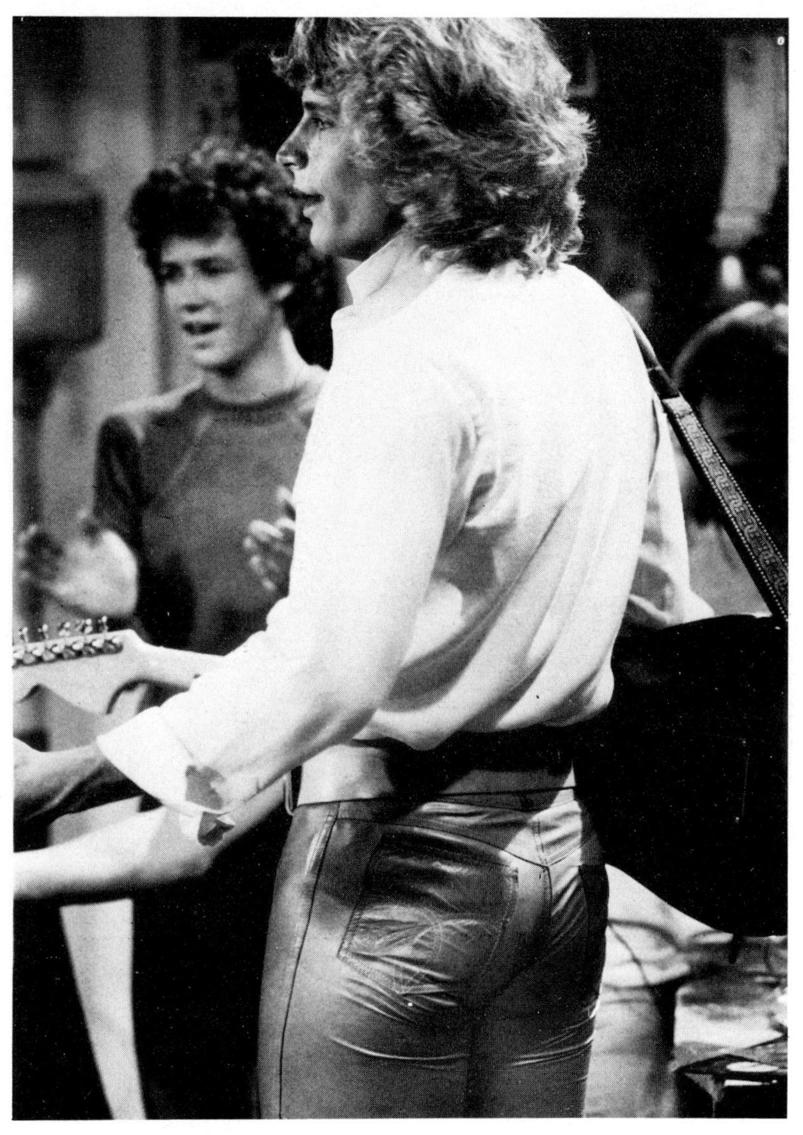

REX SMITH/Sooner or Later, he'll Take Your Breath Away

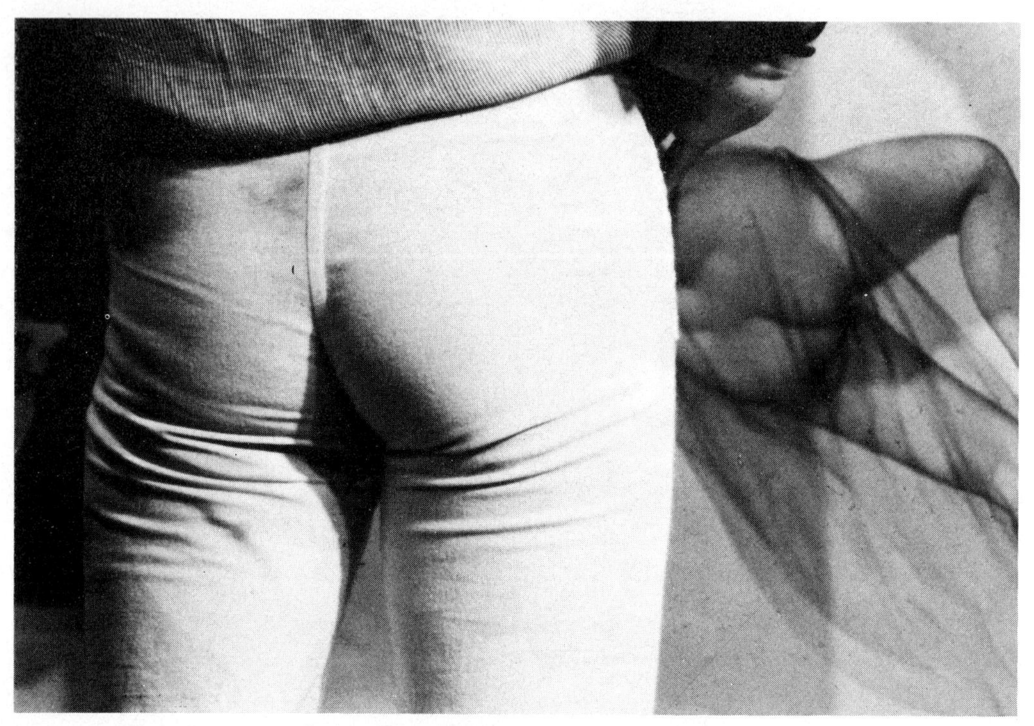

Shopping for a good piece of art

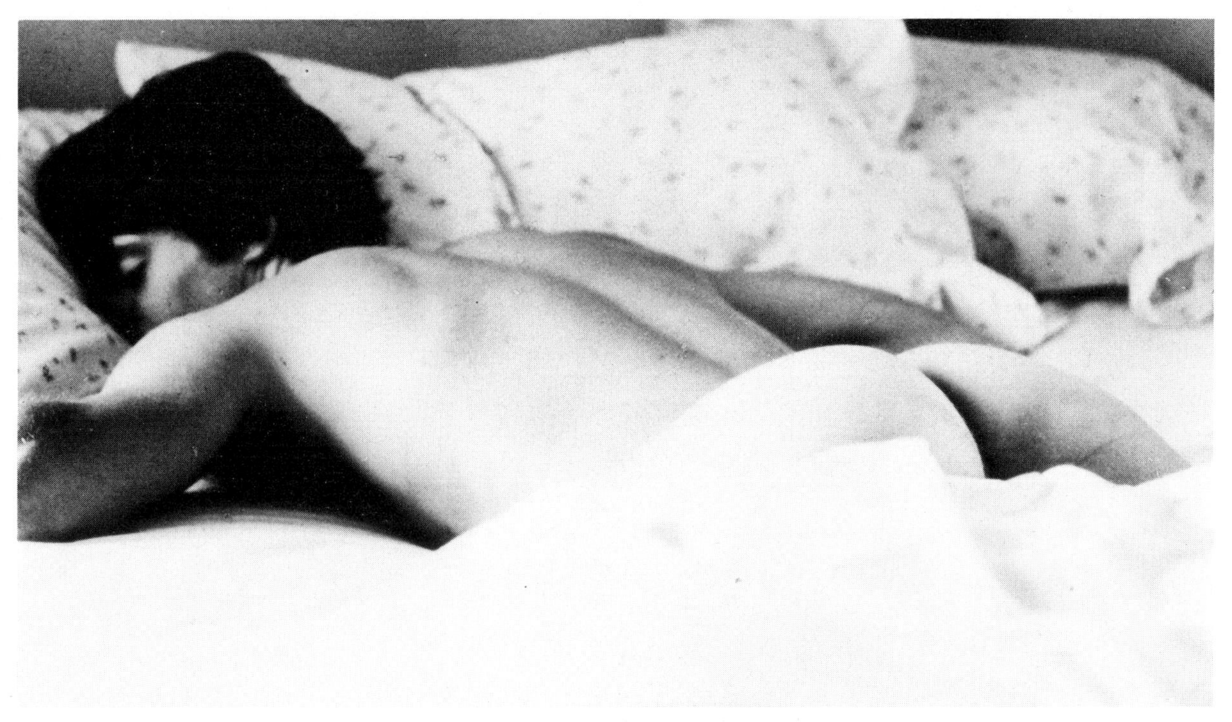

CHRIS/English Muffins

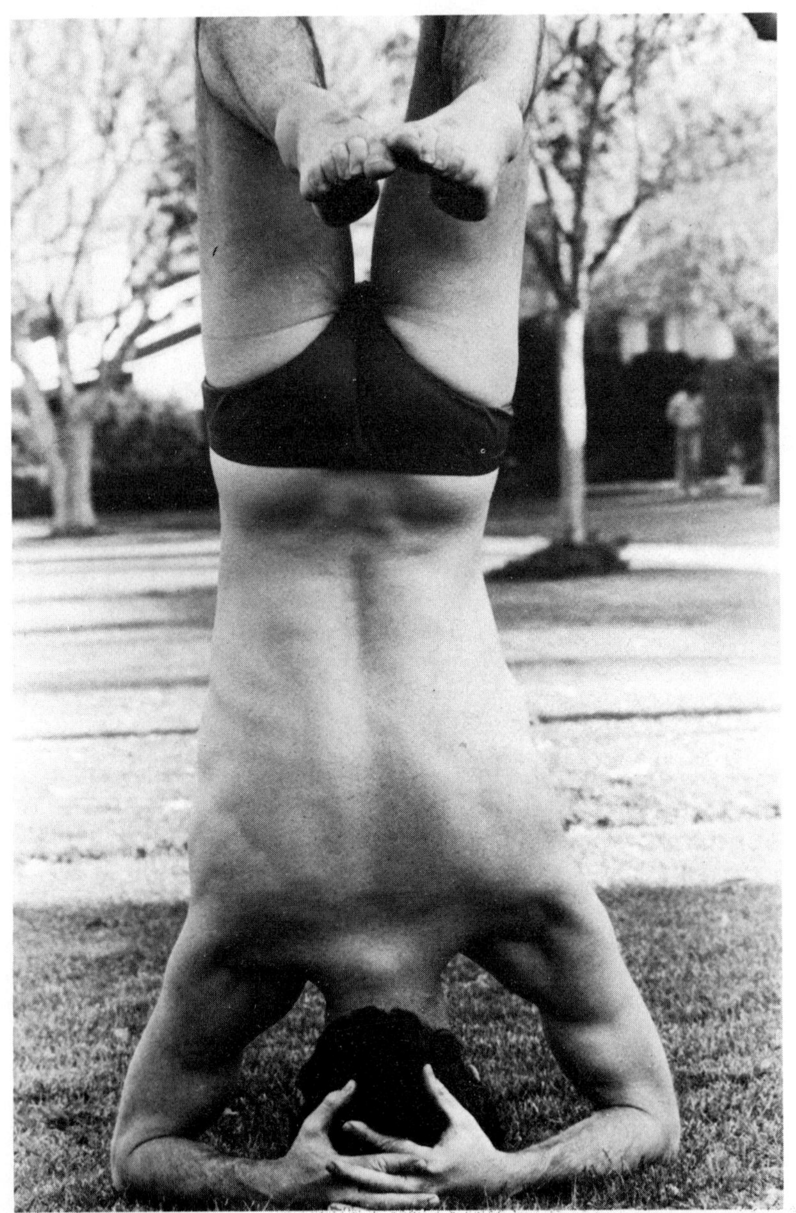

TERRY/*teacher*

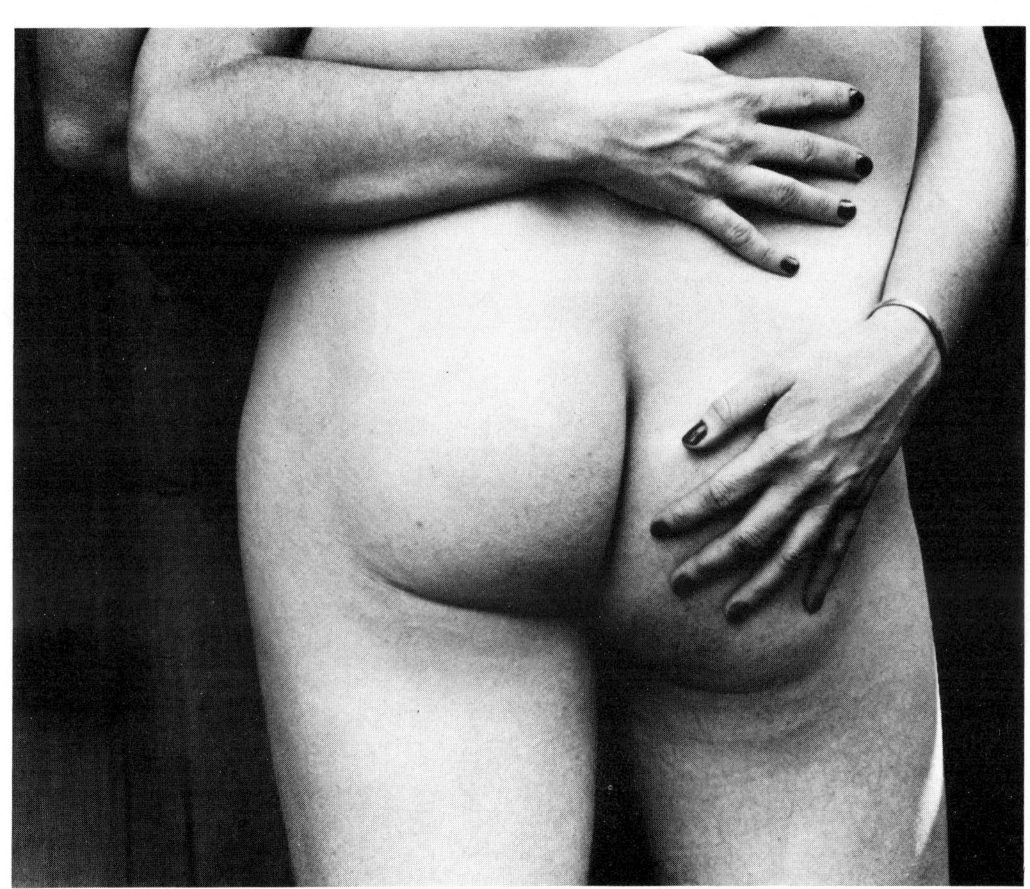

Debbie's hands

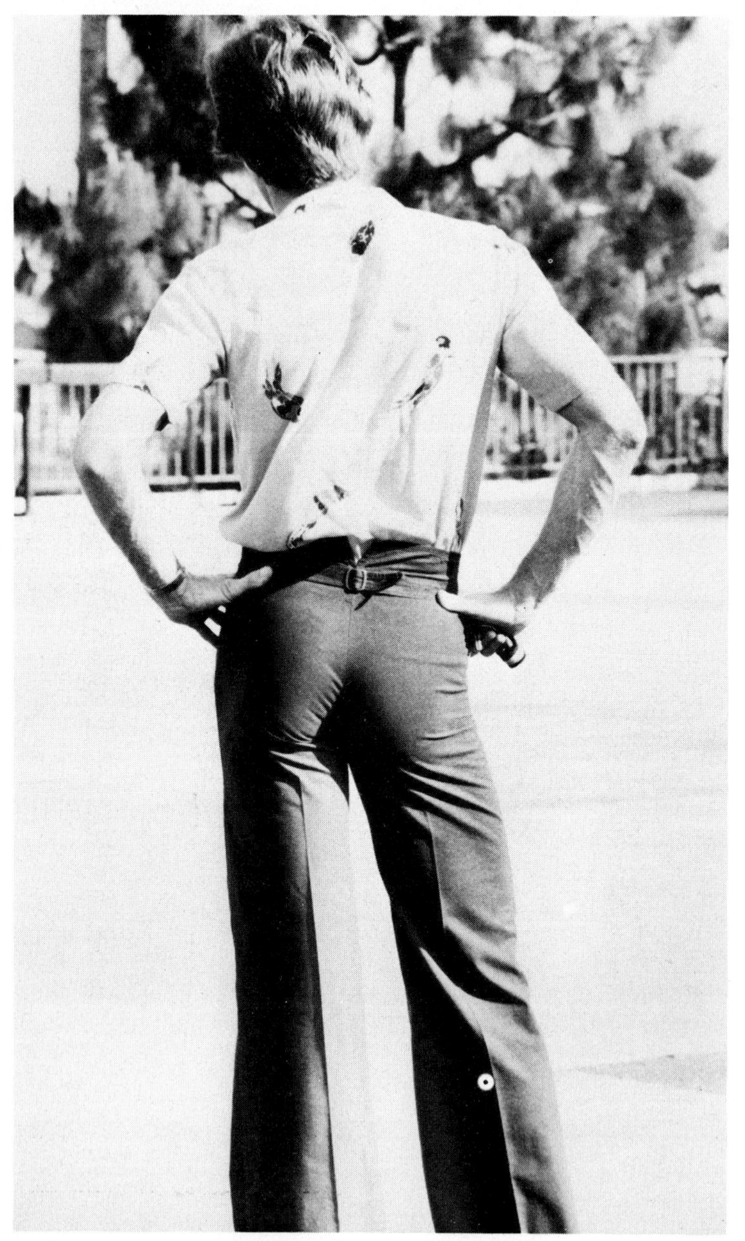

DWIGHT

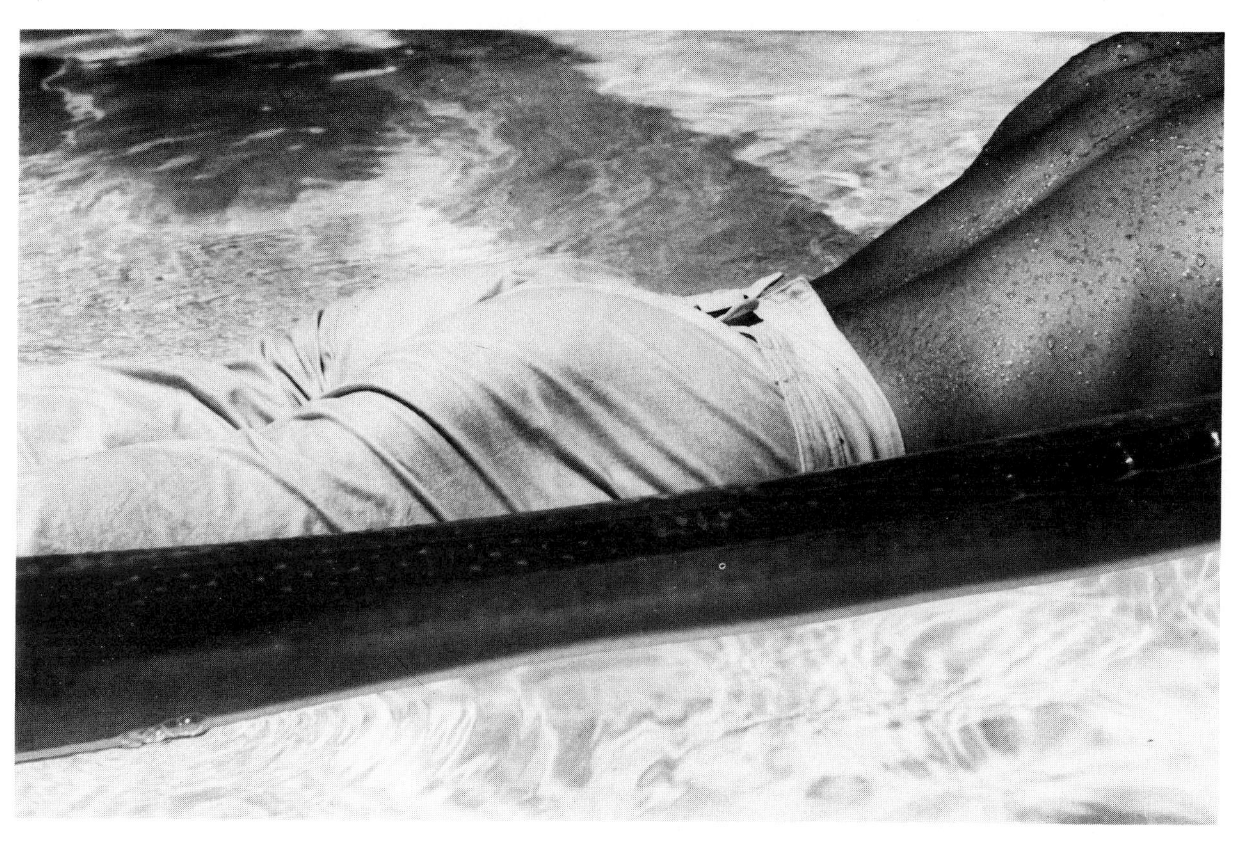

JOHN

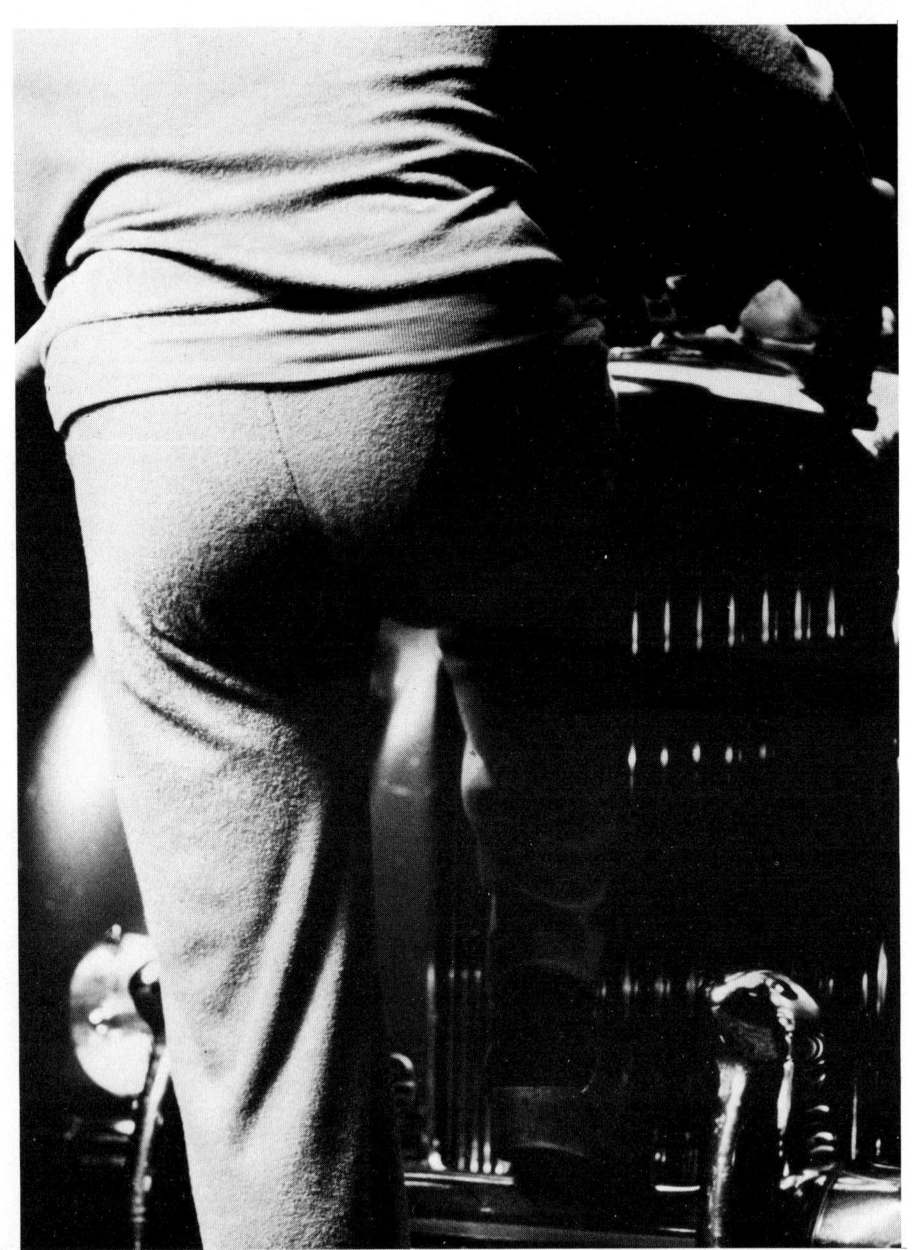

SUGAR DADDY

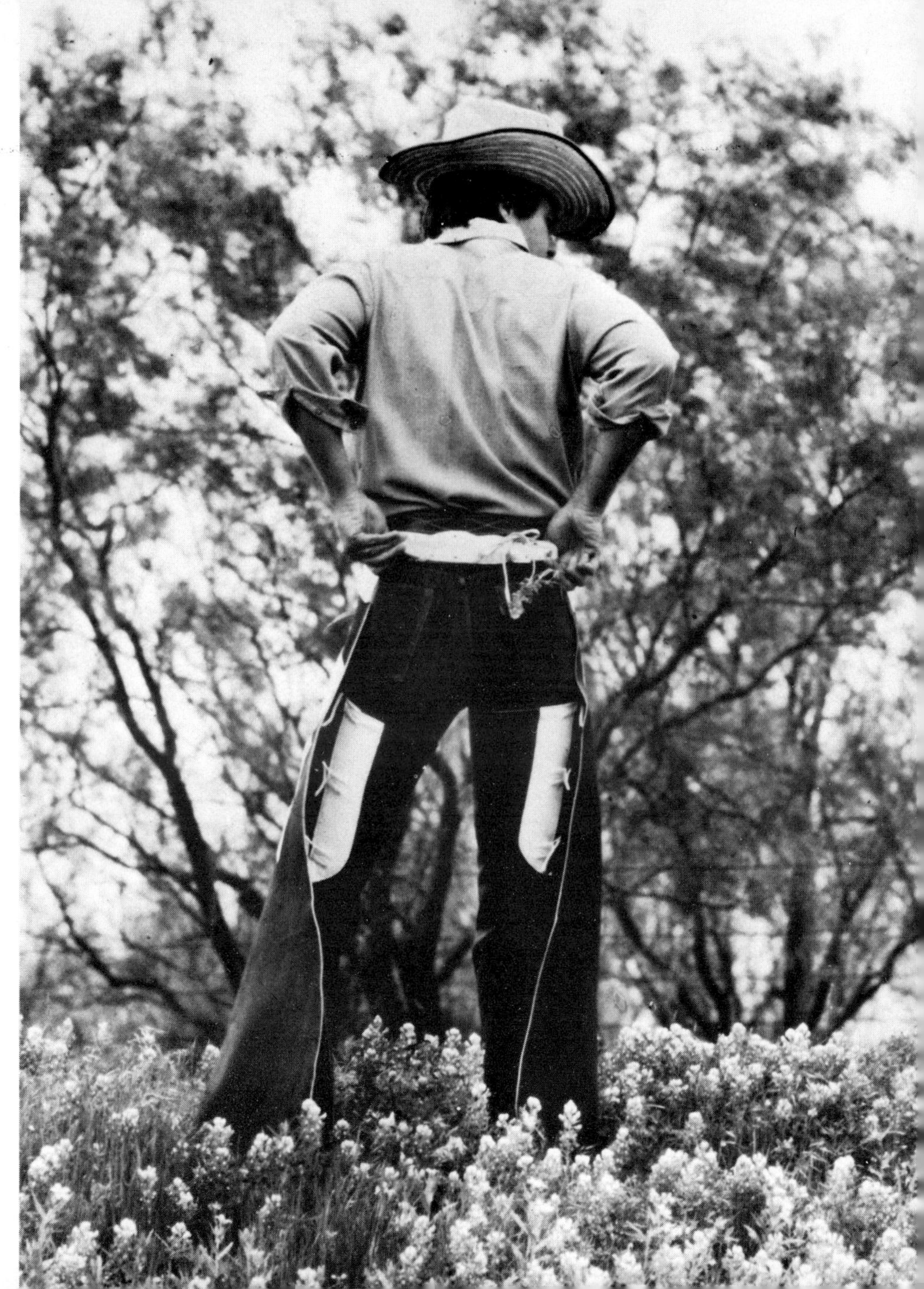

RALPH

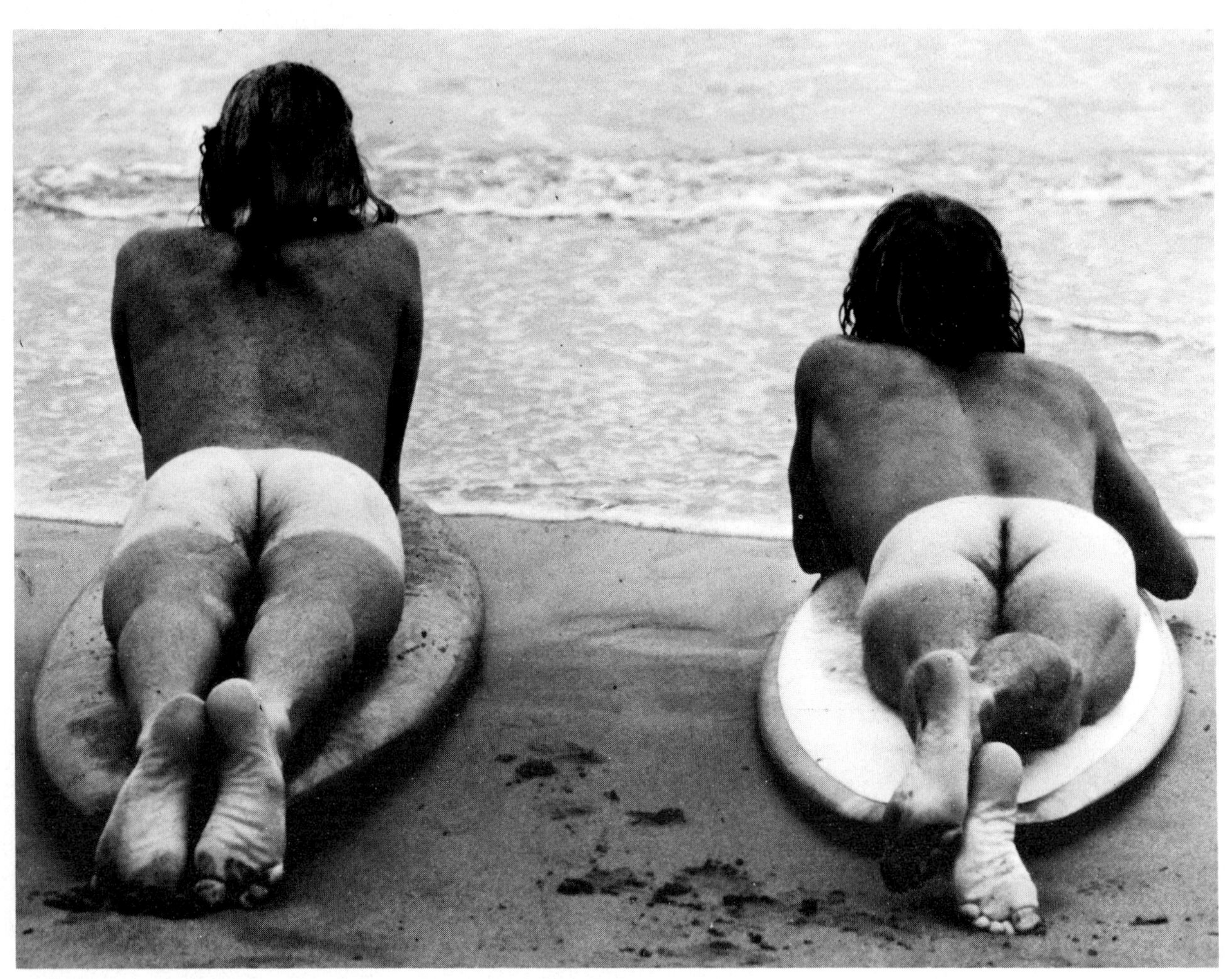

STEVE and DAVID/artists

JOSH TAYLOR/Star of
Days of Our Lives *(NBC) . . .*
and he used to play darn
good football!

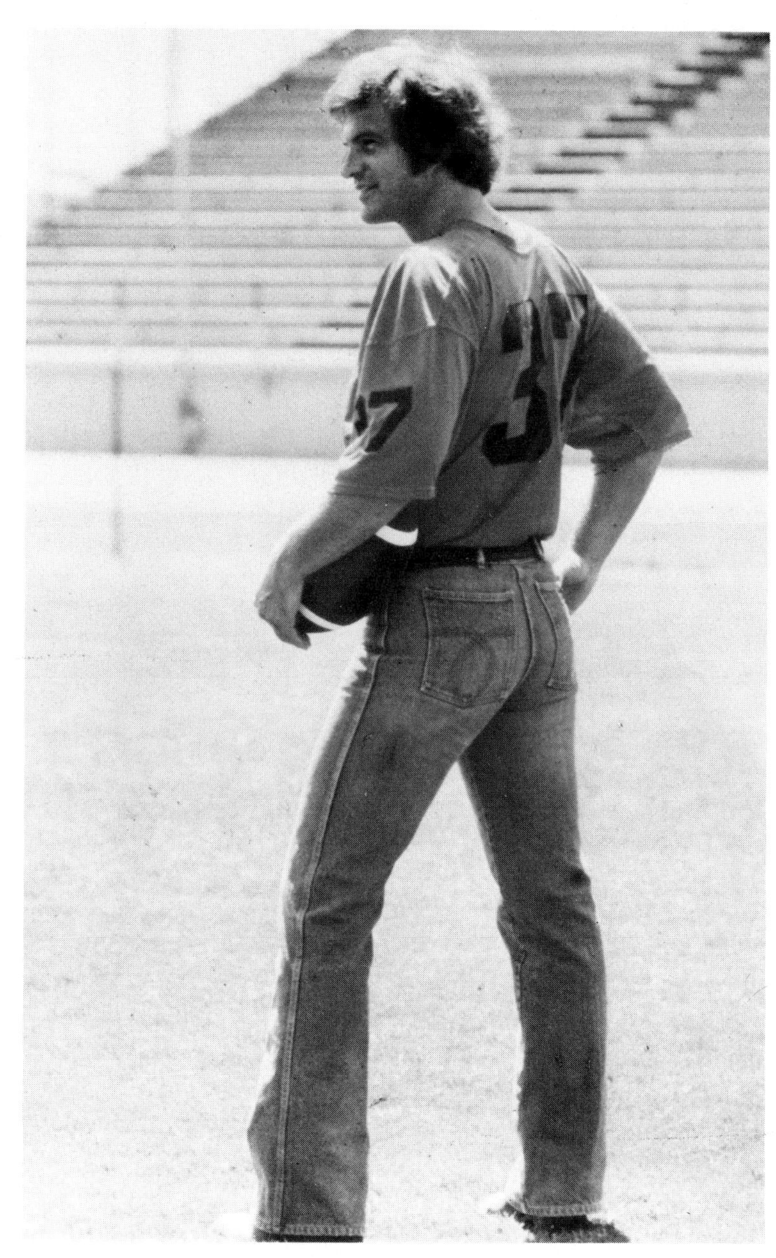

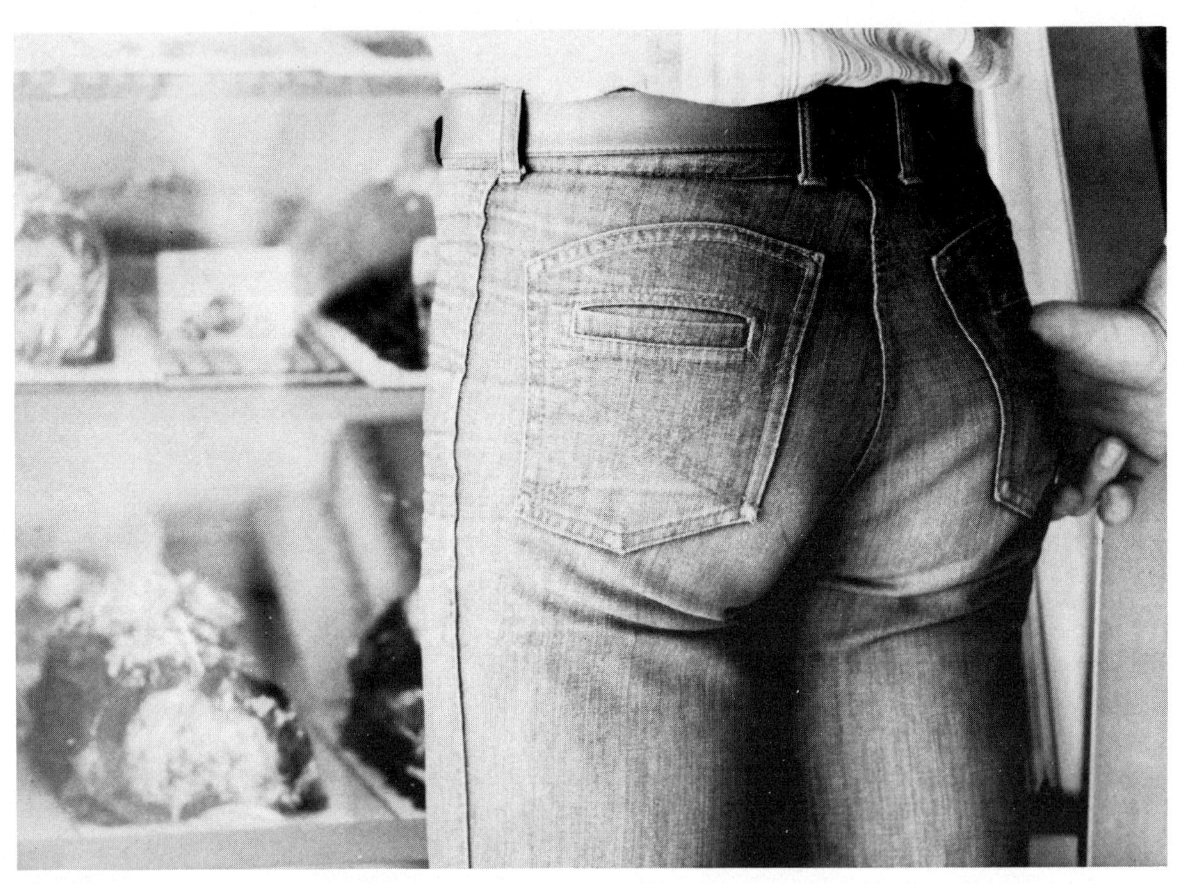

TERRENCE/actor

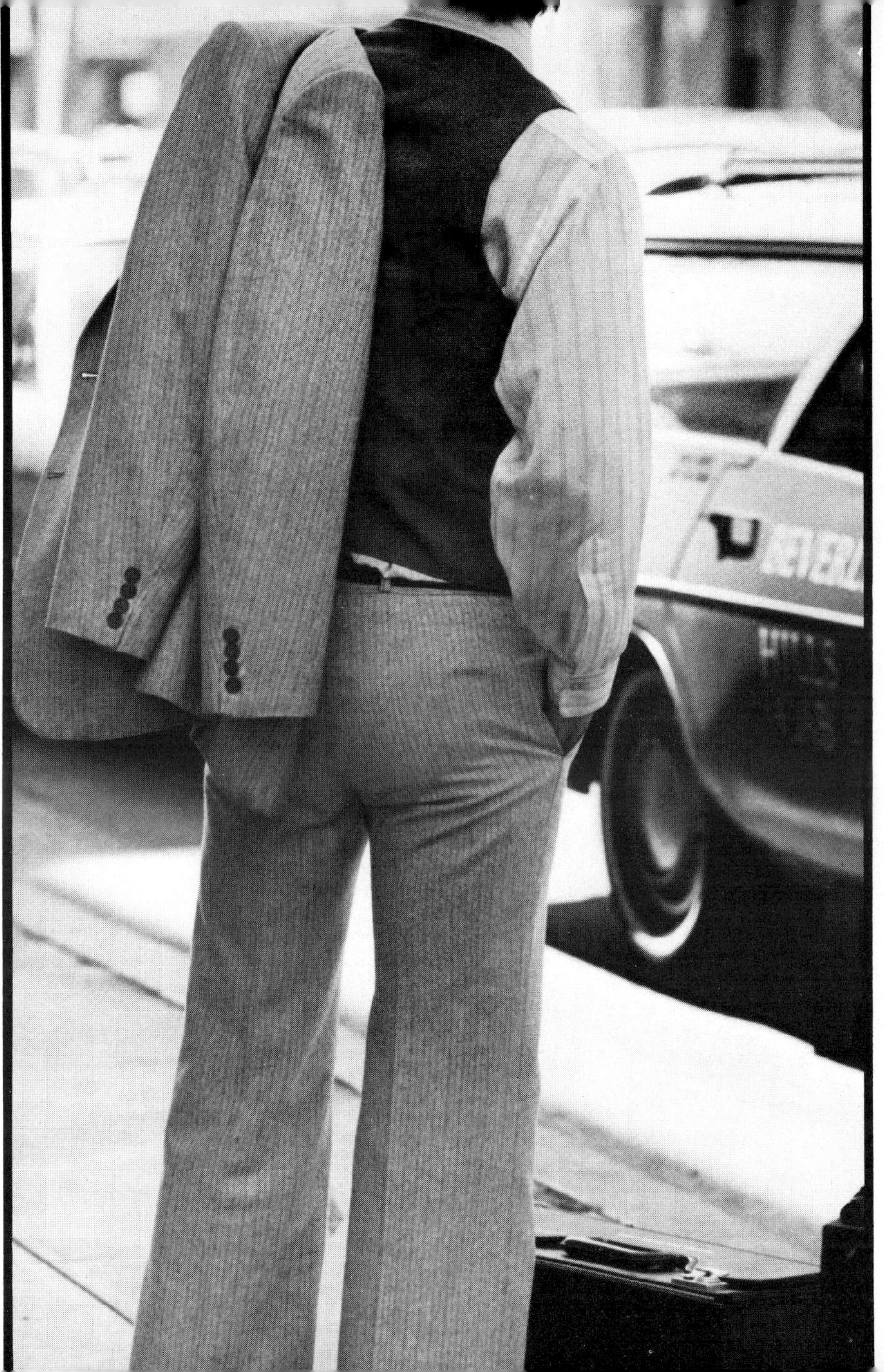

MEN AT WORK

BOB/lawyer

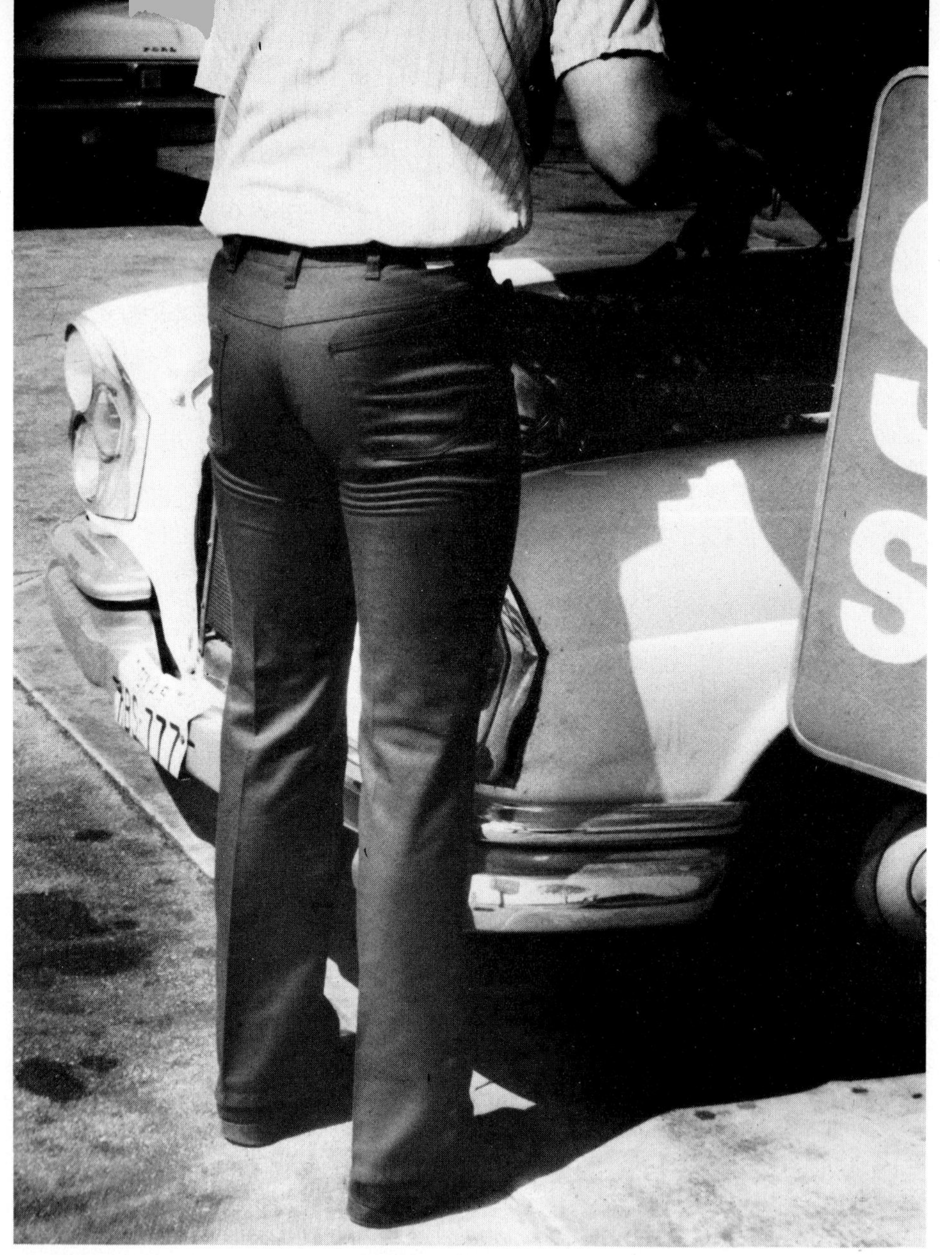

TONY

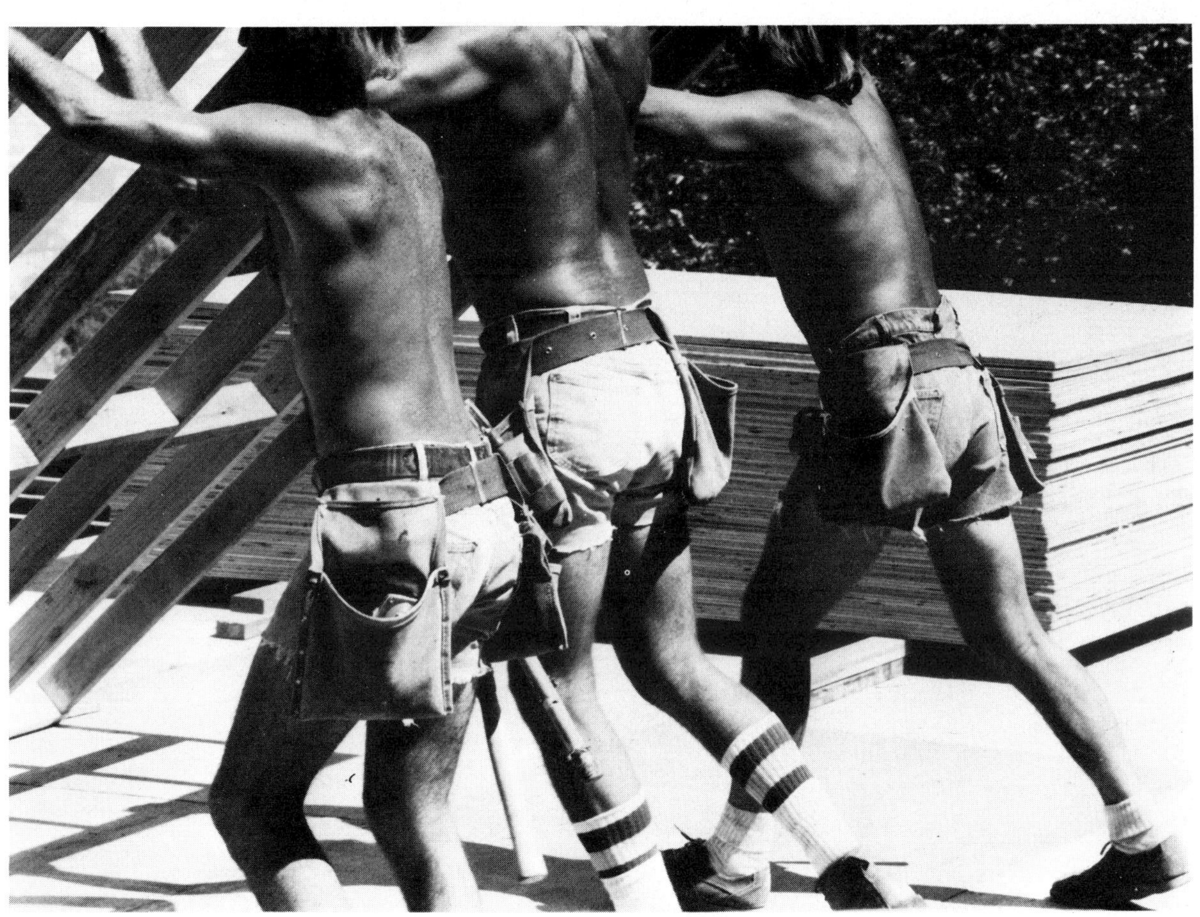

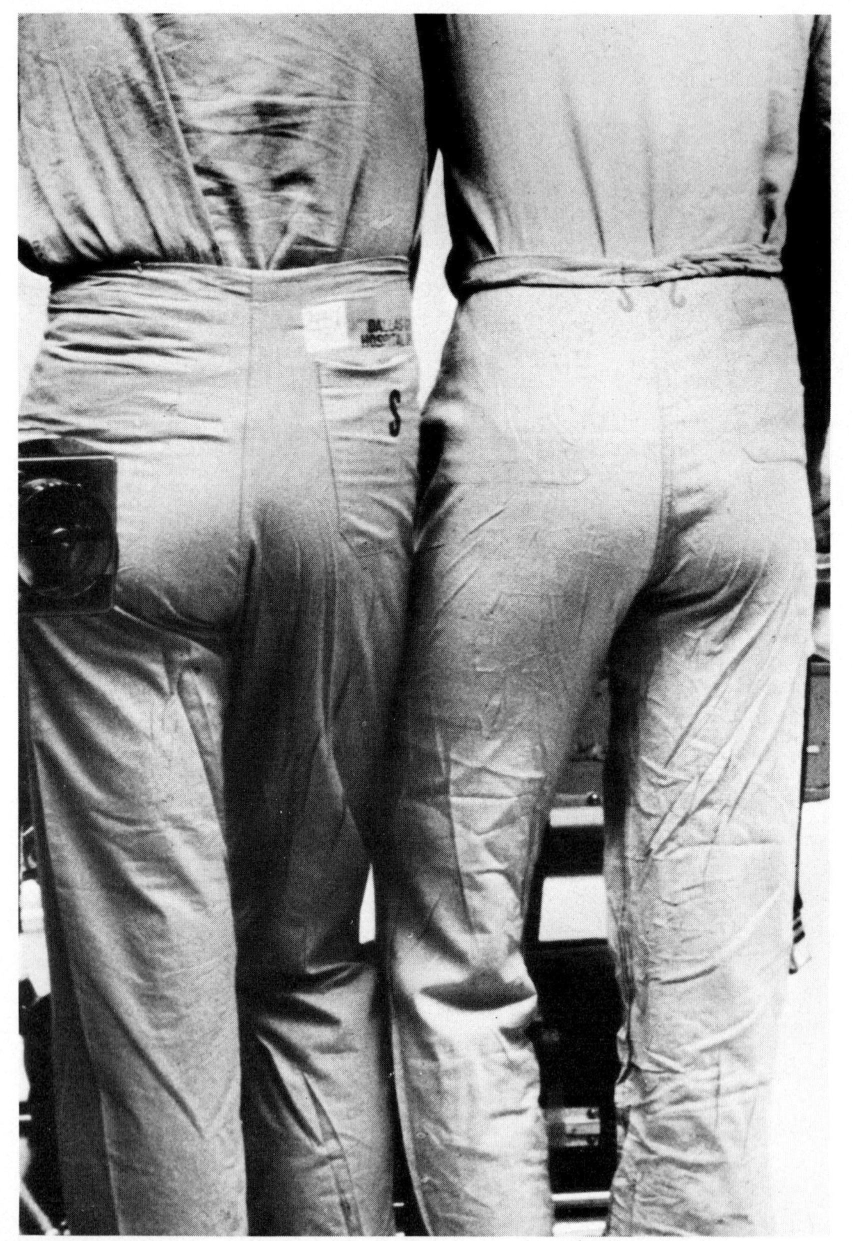

Dr. ERJ and med. student

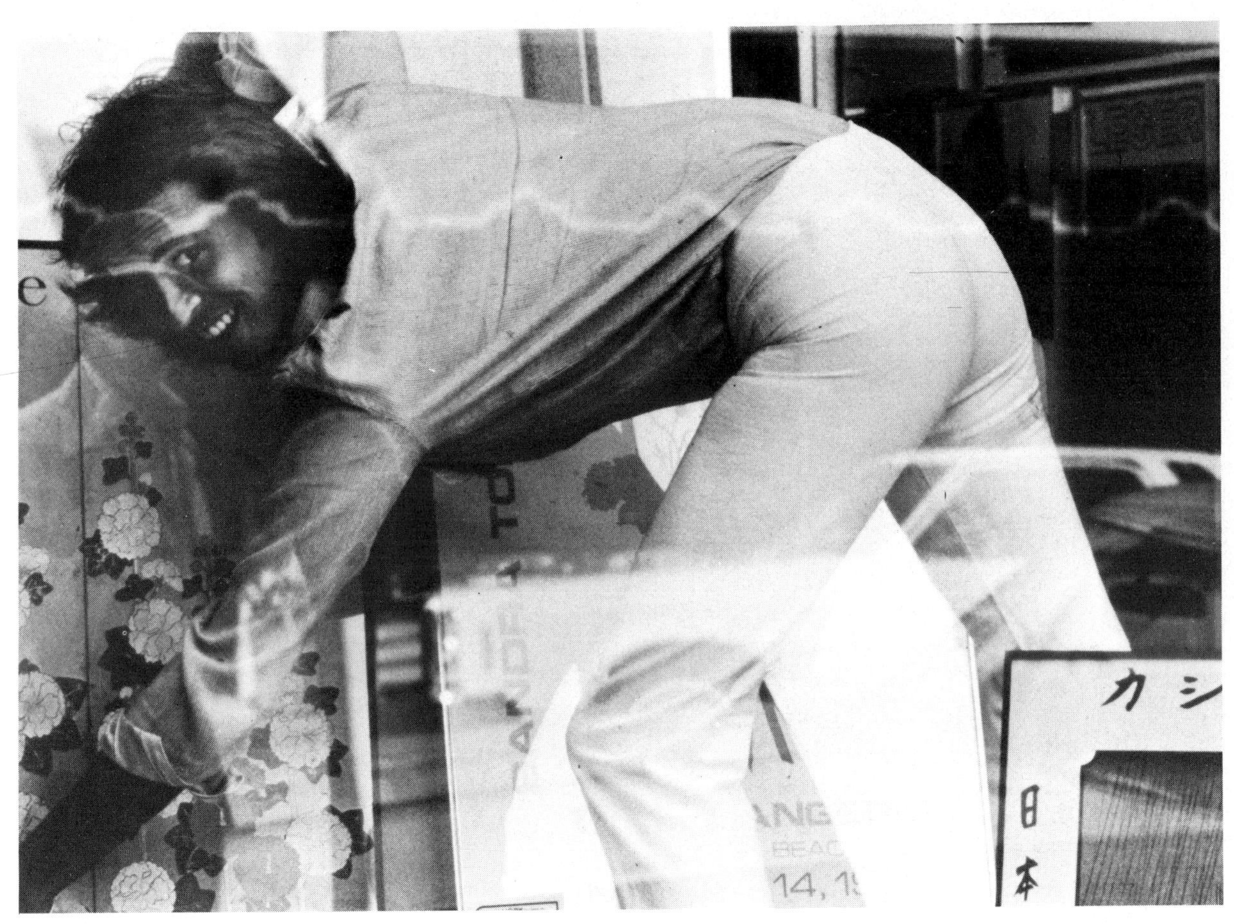

SHELLY

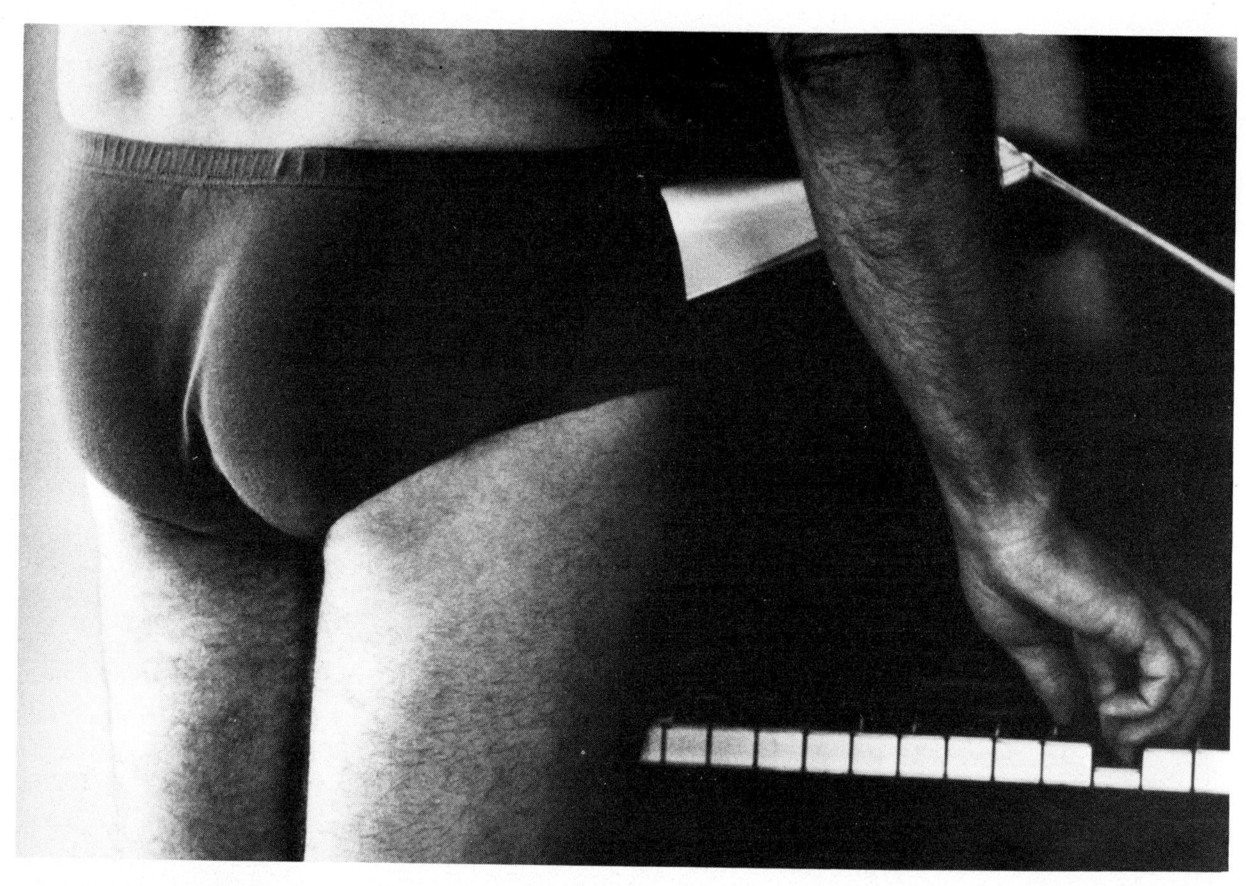

SONNY BONO

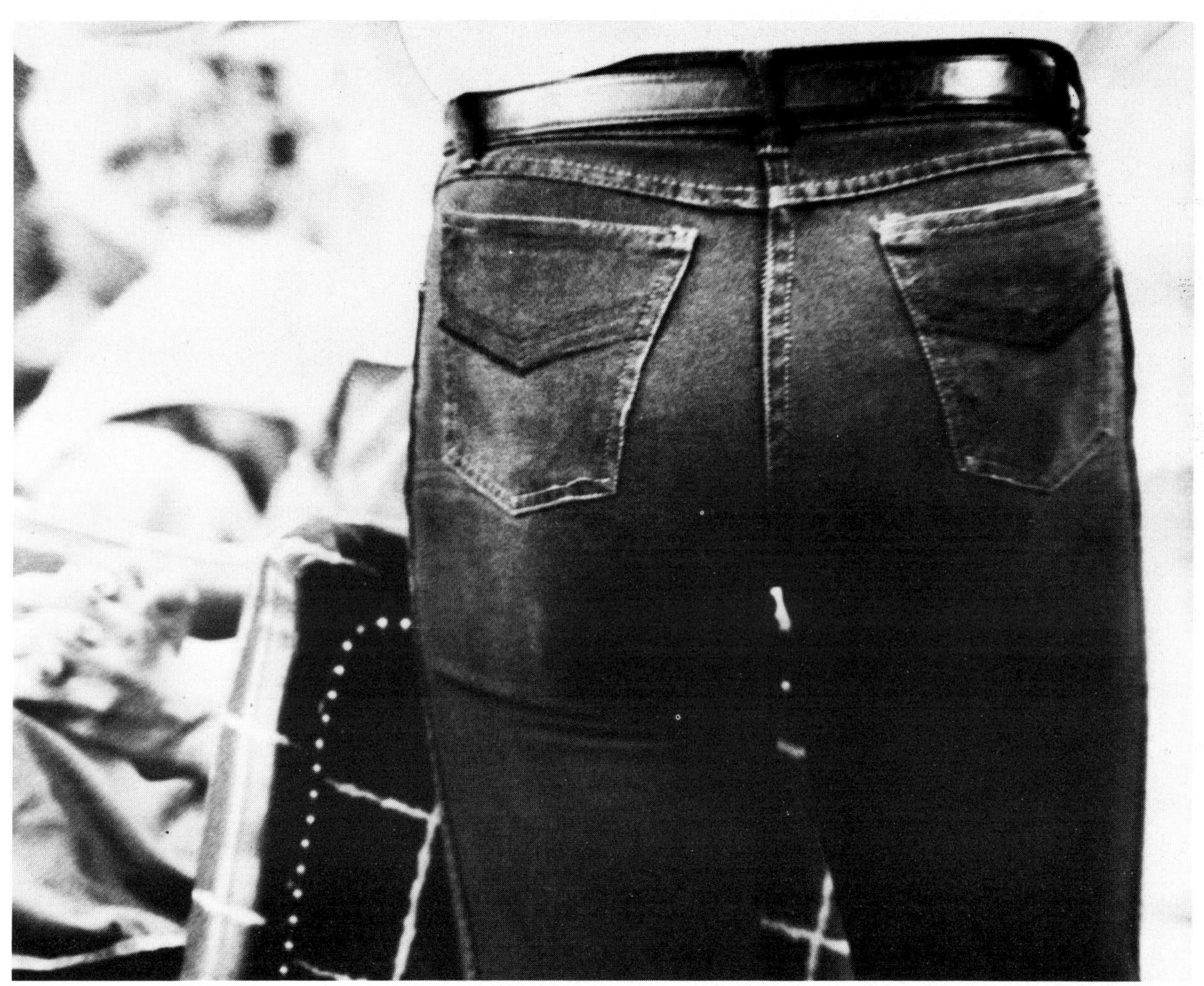

KALE/hairdresser

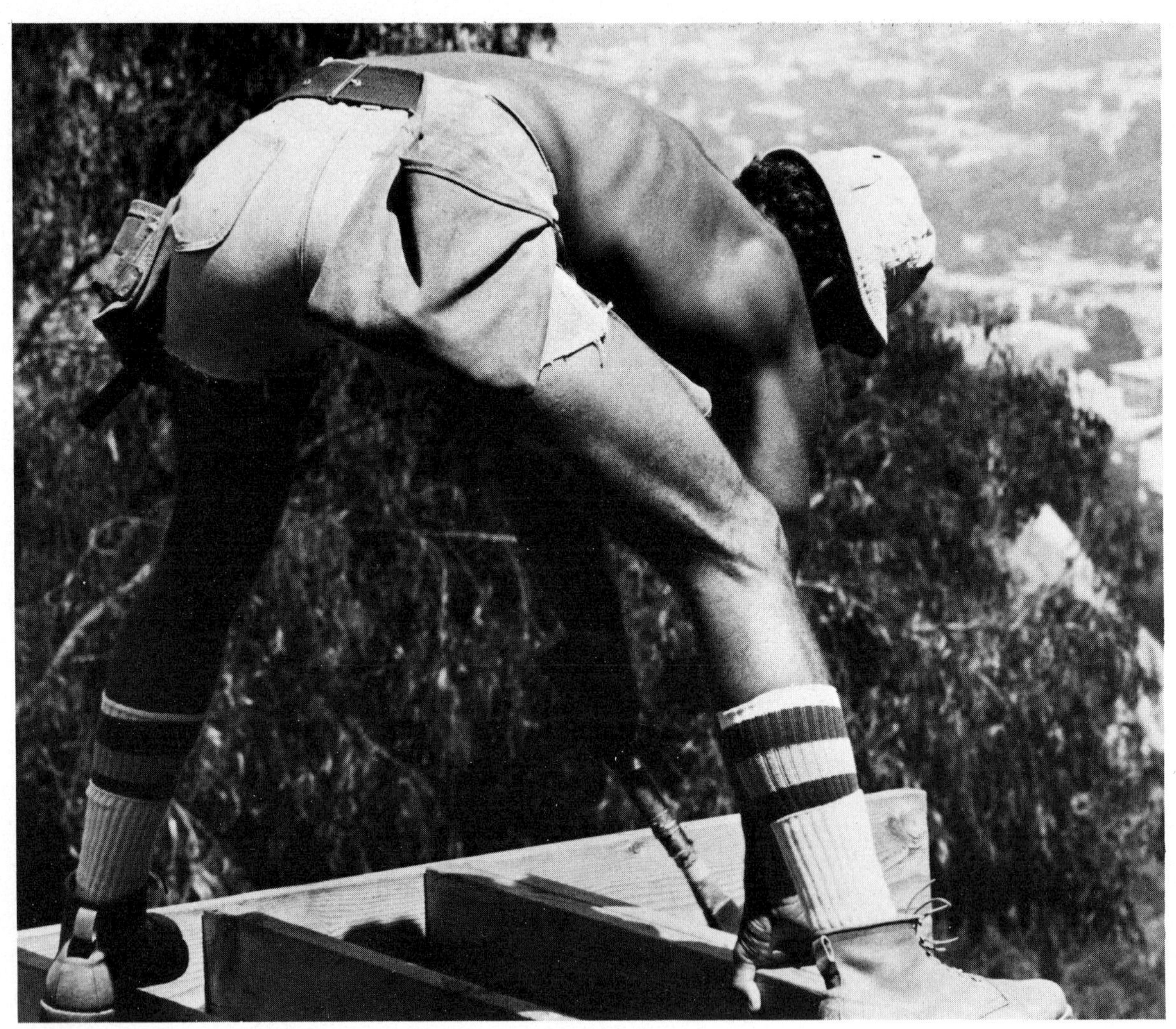

MIKE/builder
A house with a view

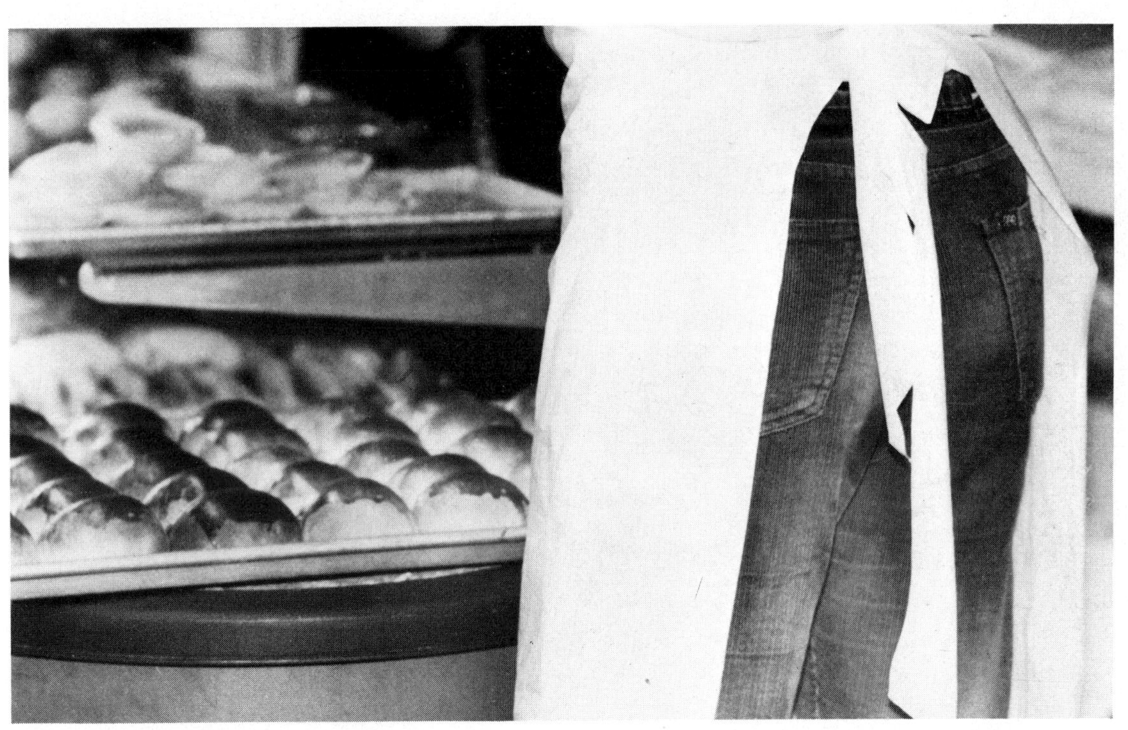

Chinatown bakery

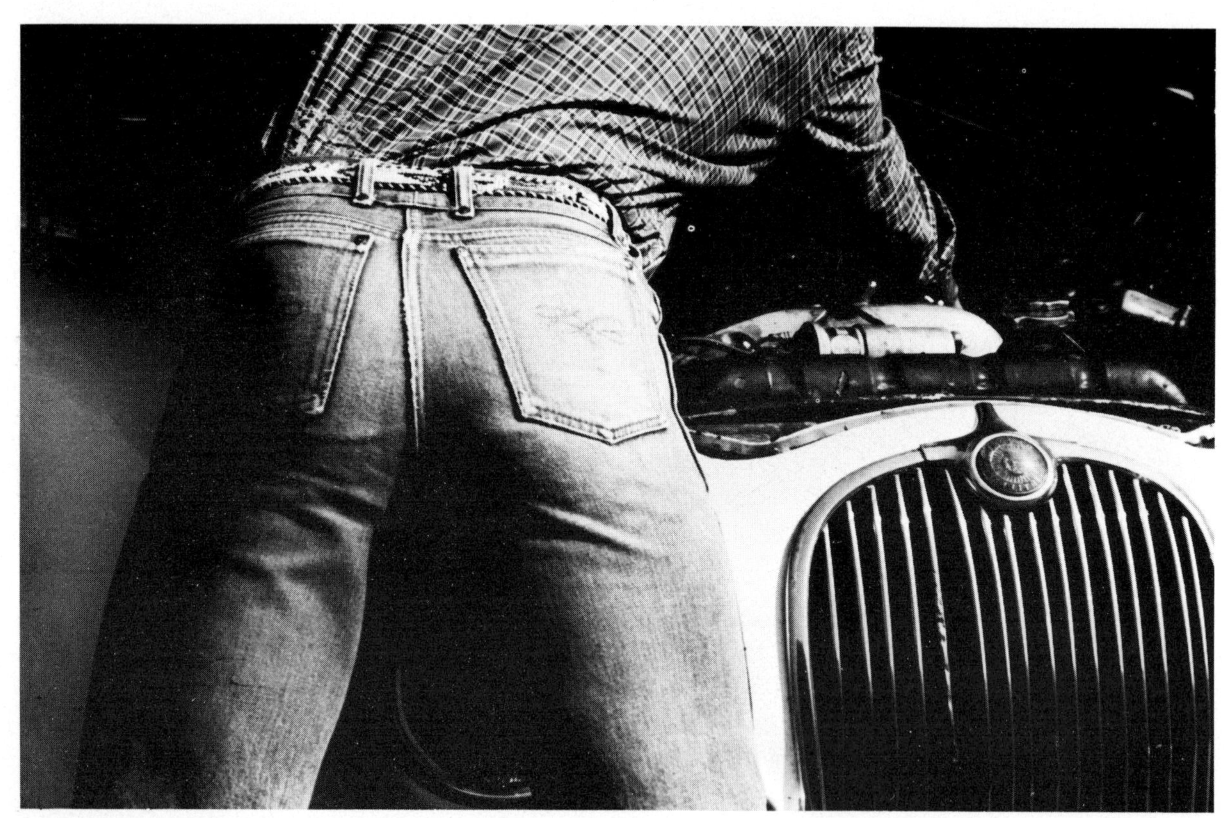

ALEXANDER

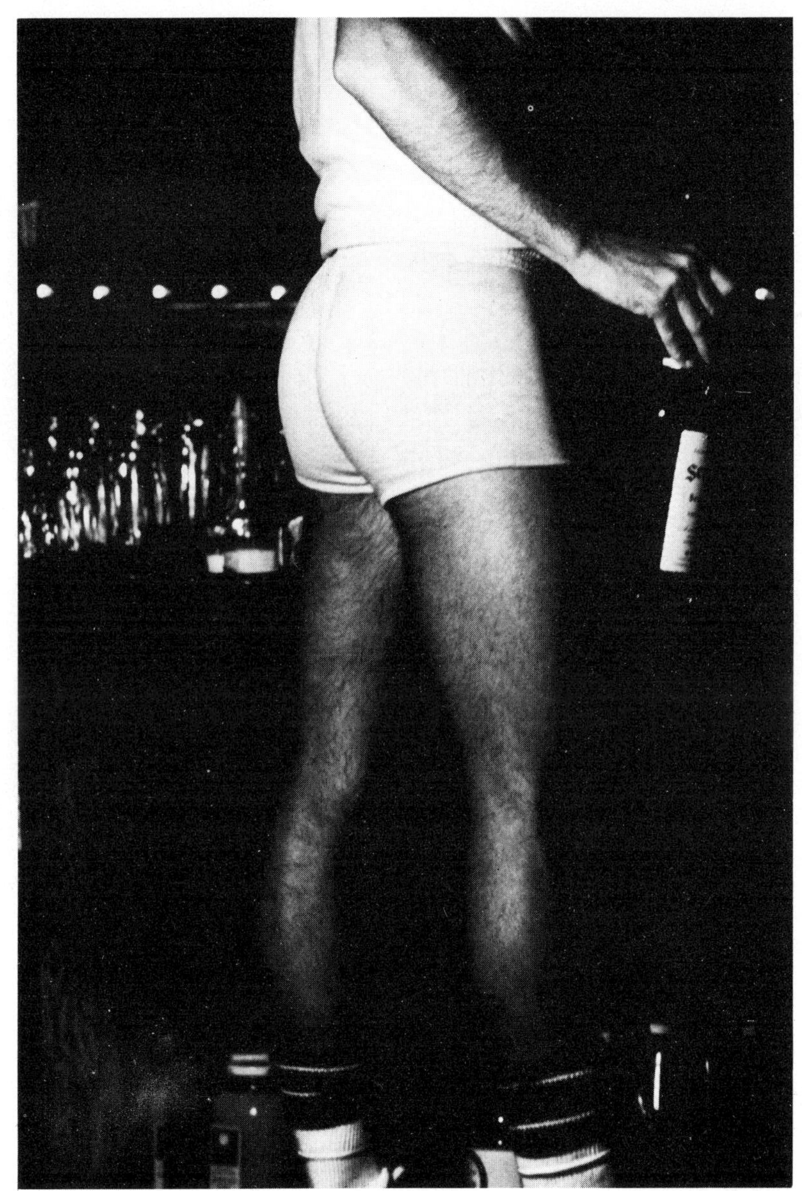

DAVID/bartender

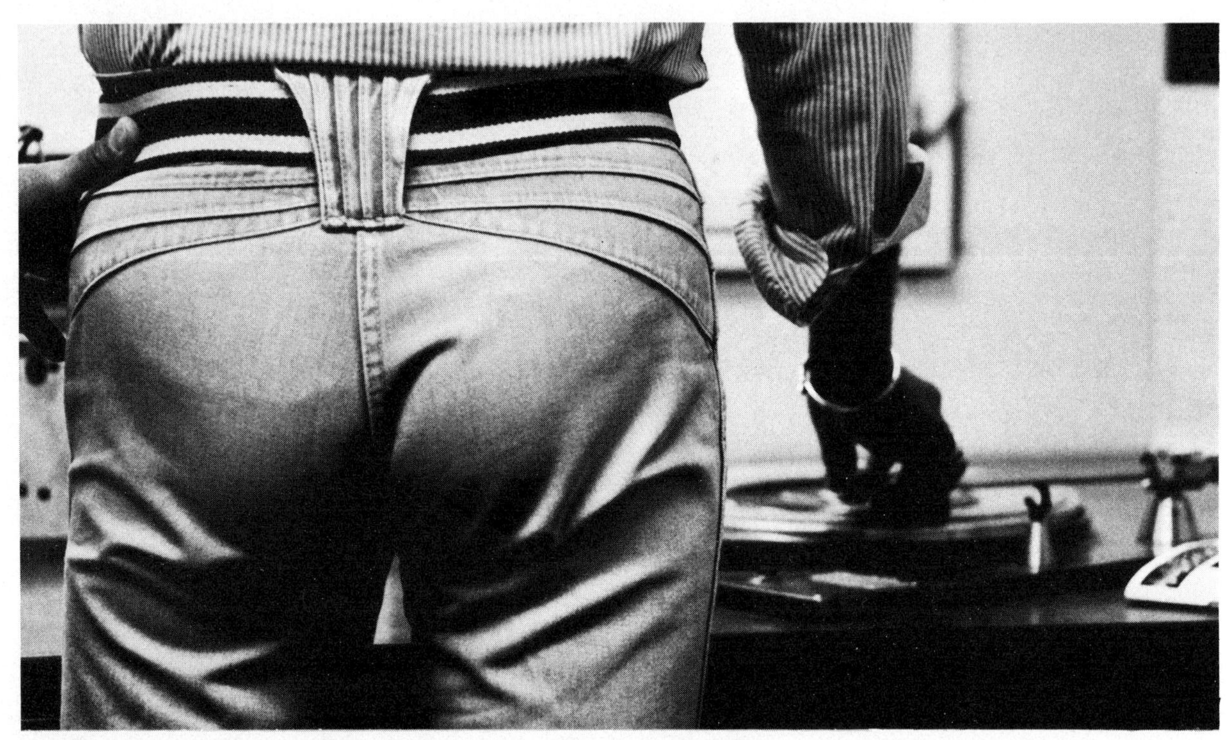

GEOFF EDWARDS/television and radio personality

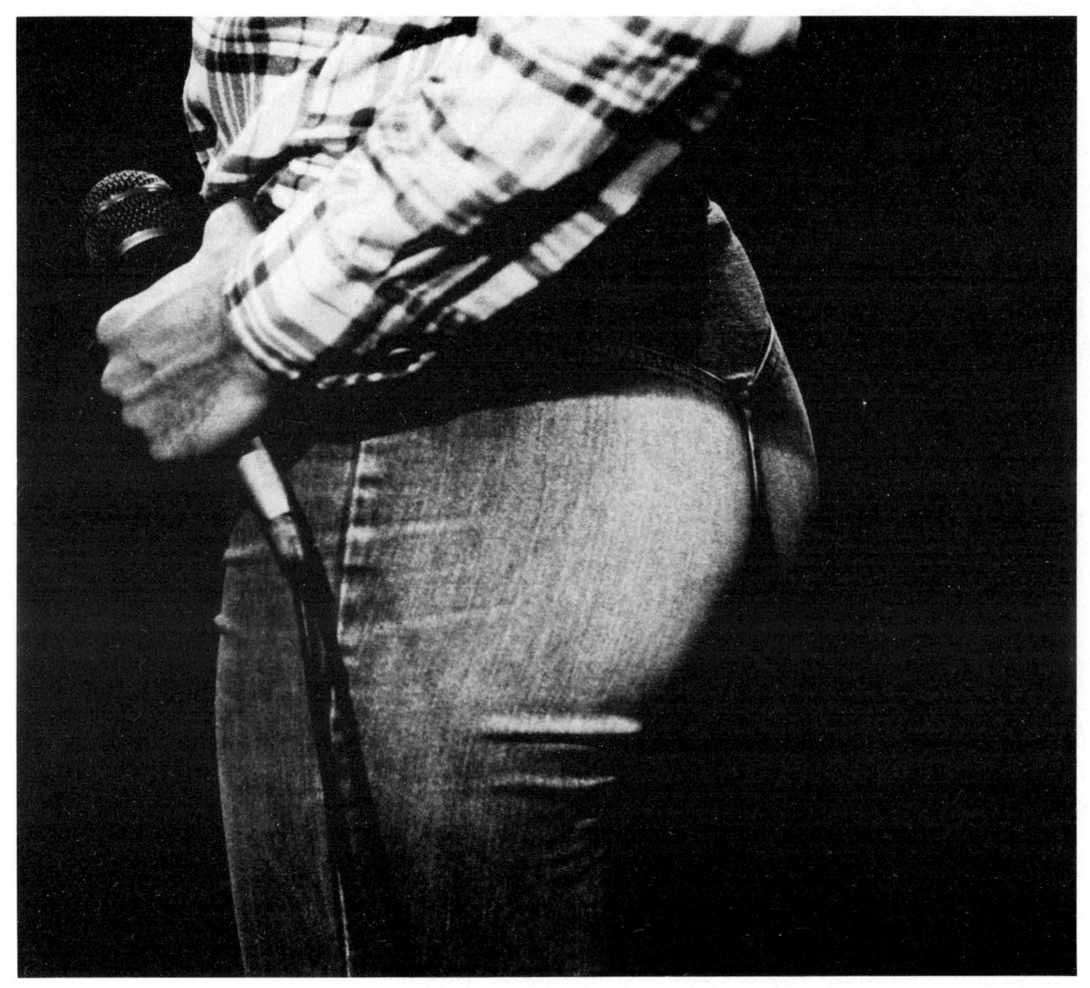

MARK/singer

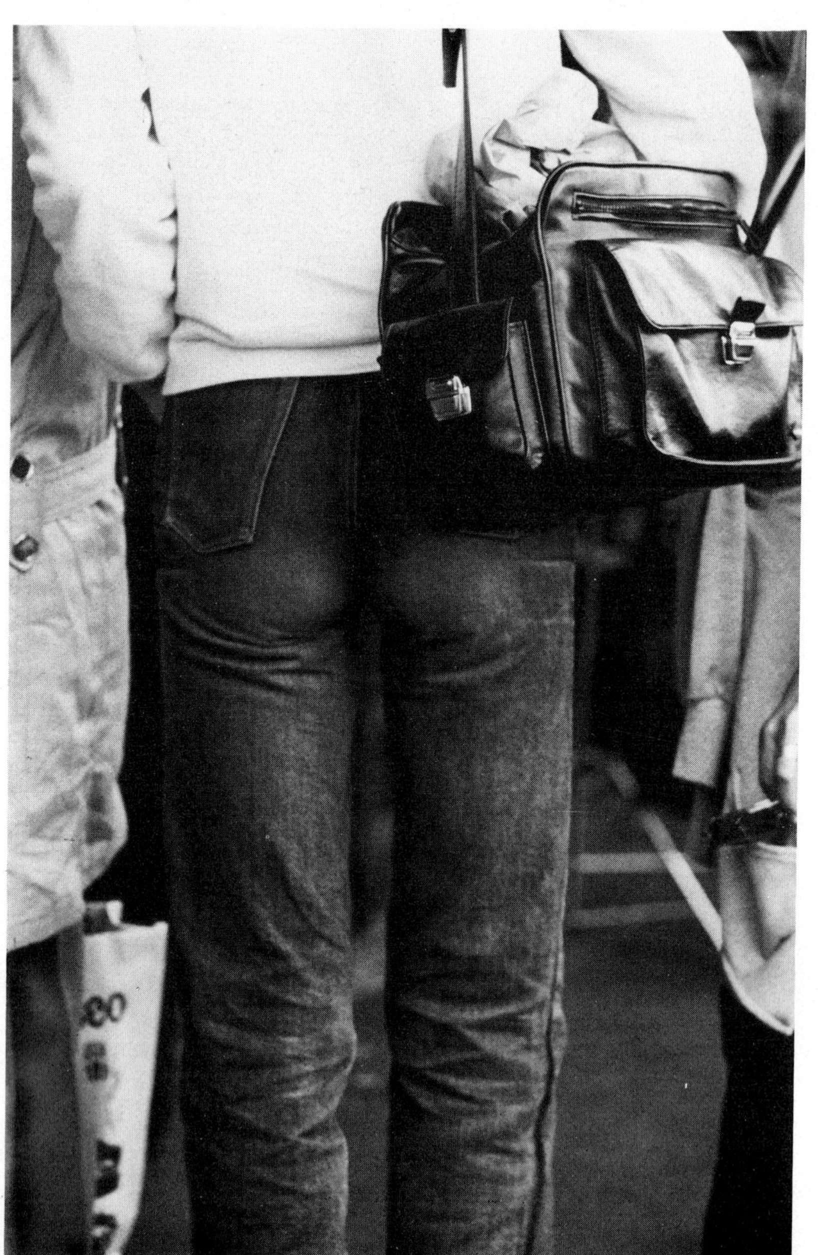

Lunch break

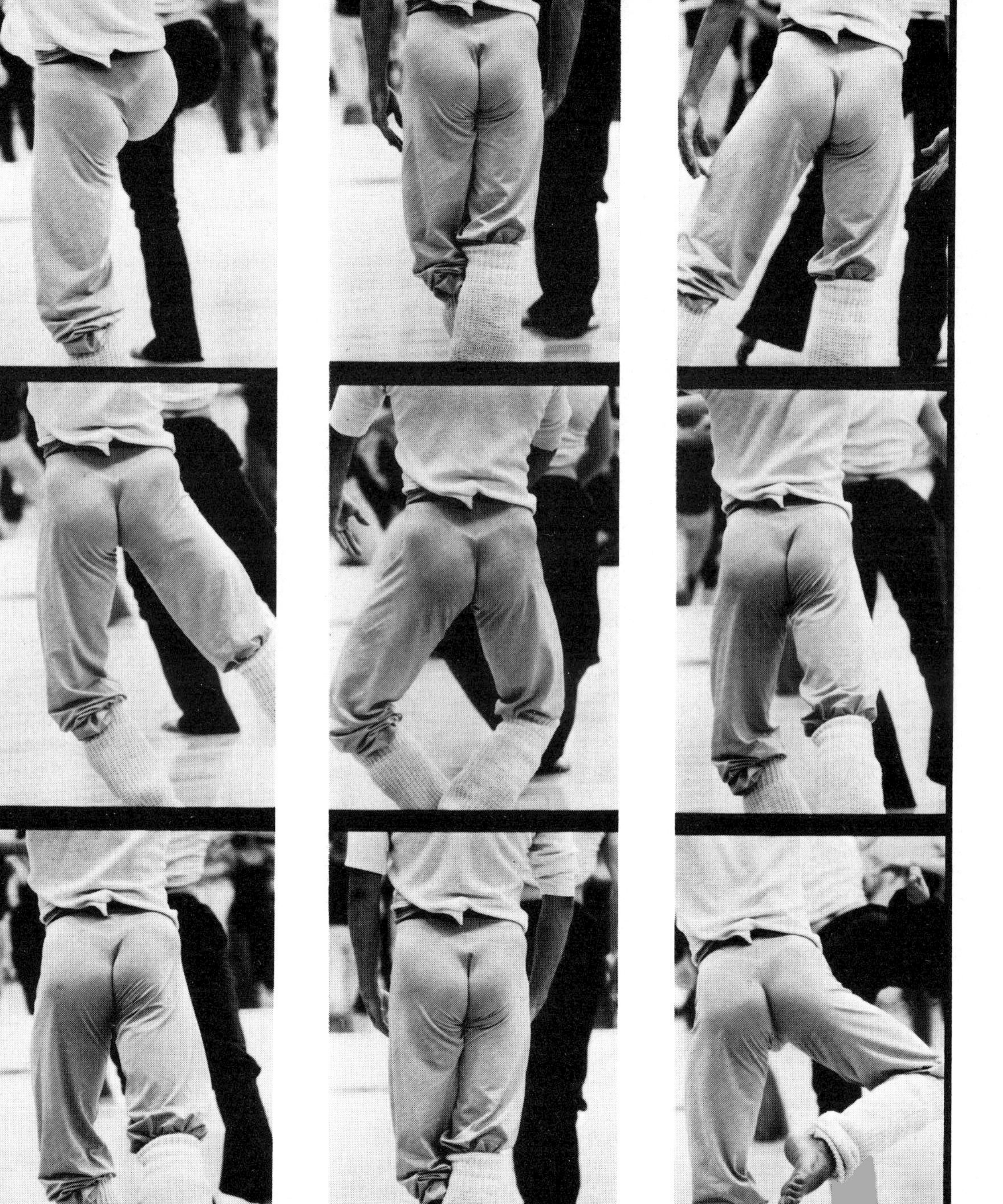

DANCERS

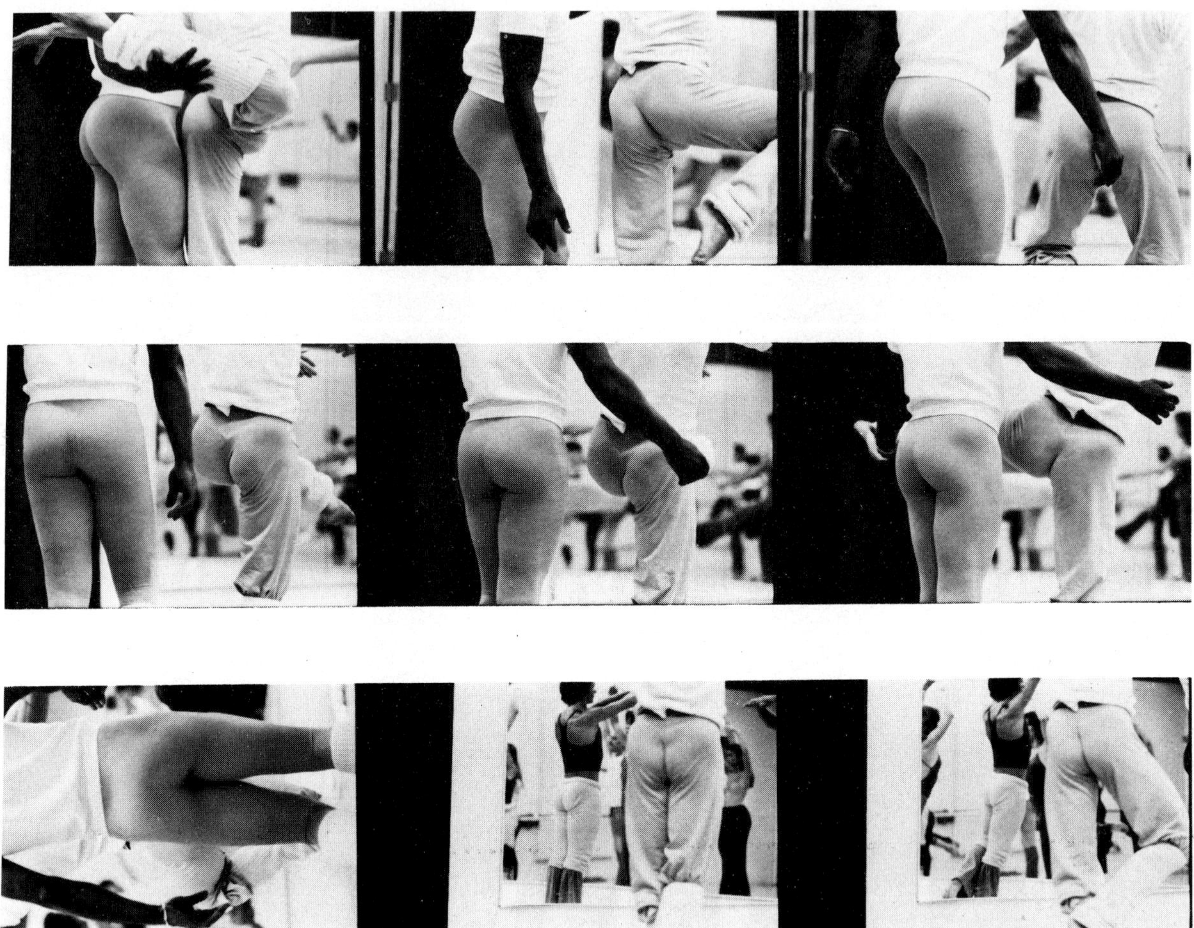

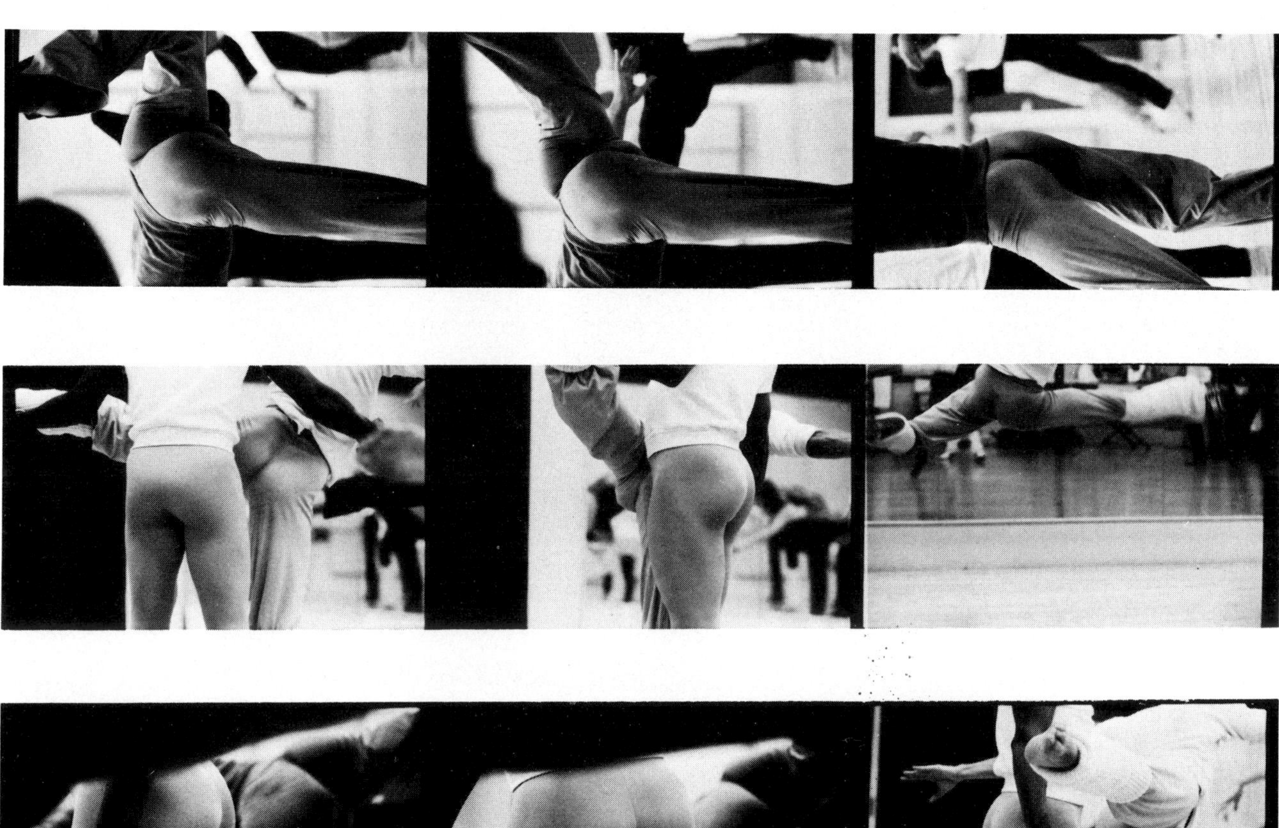

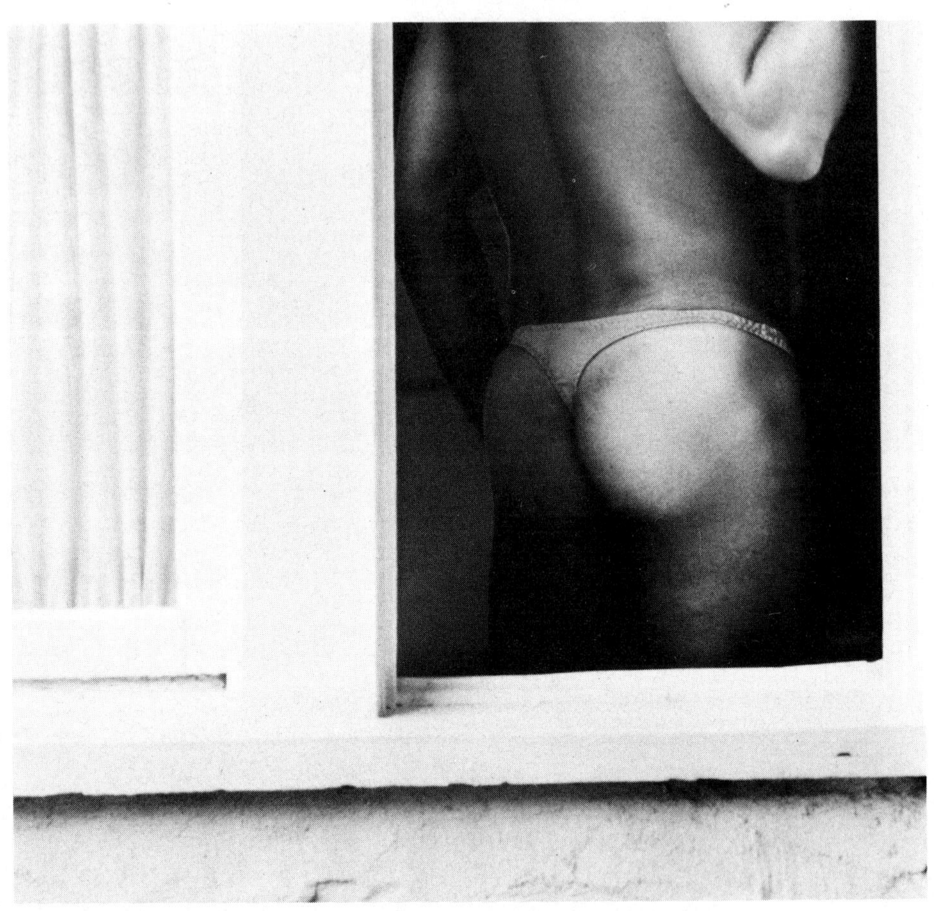

Rear window

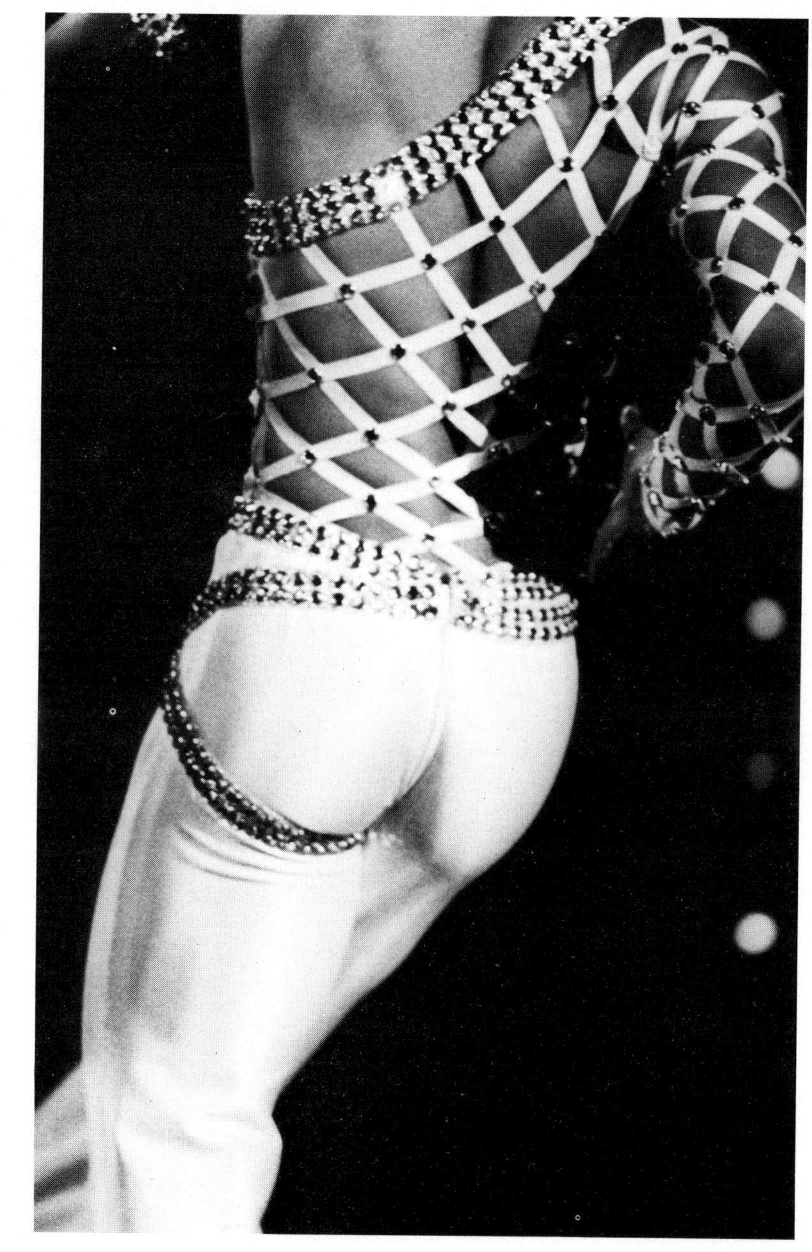

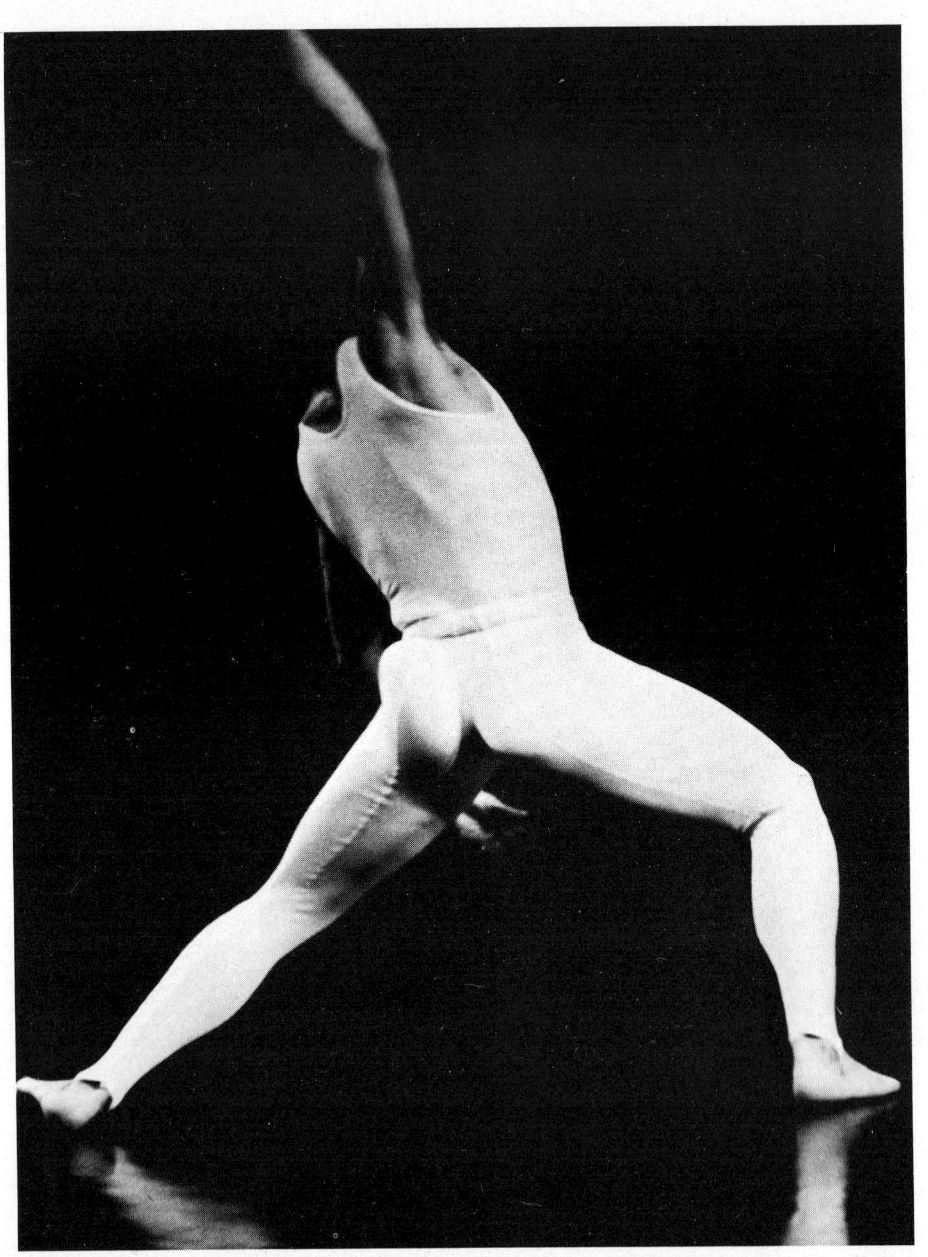

NICK GUNN/
former Paul Taylor
Principal

SPORTS

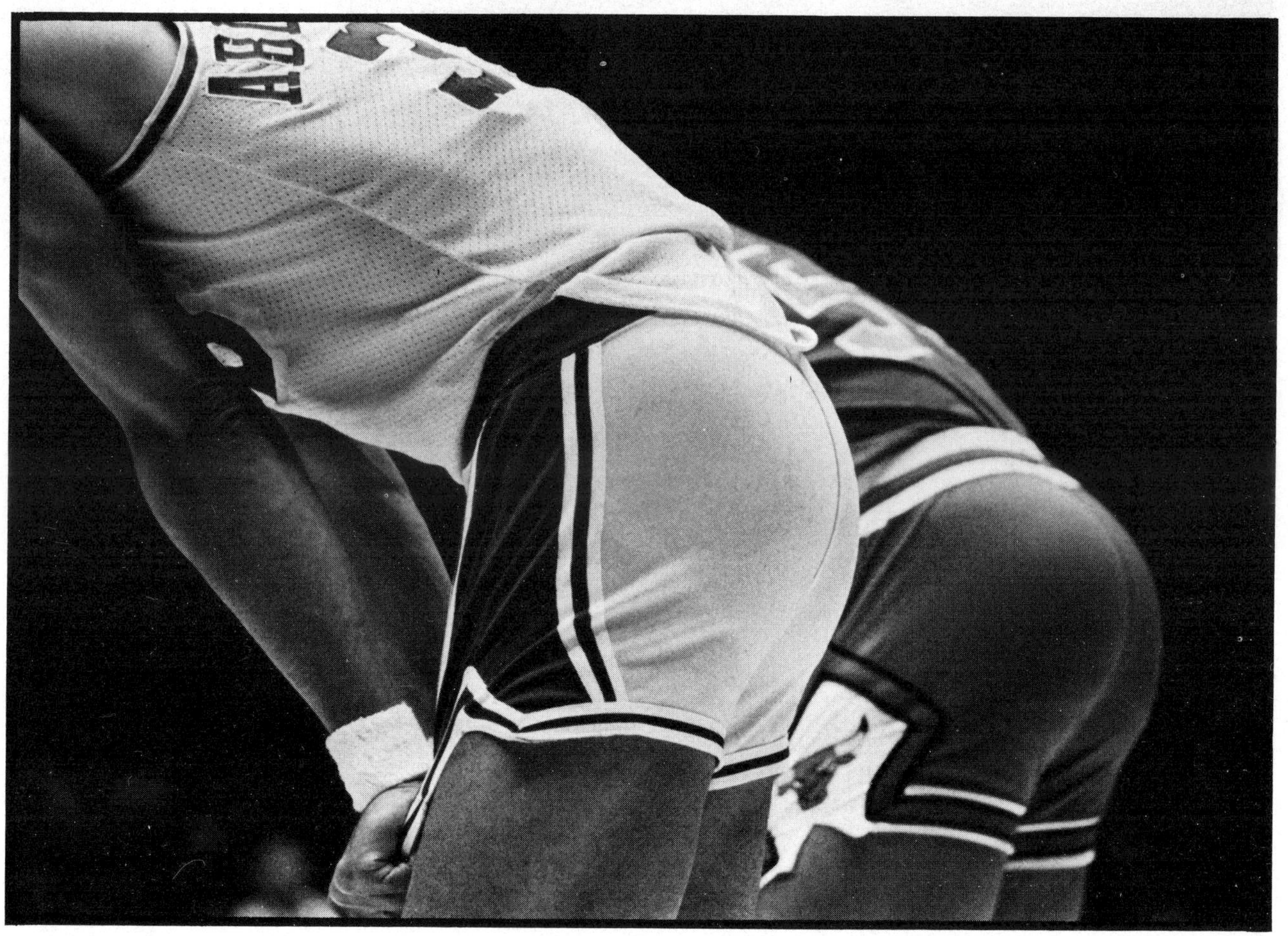

KAREEM ABDUL-JABBAR/Los Angeles Lakers

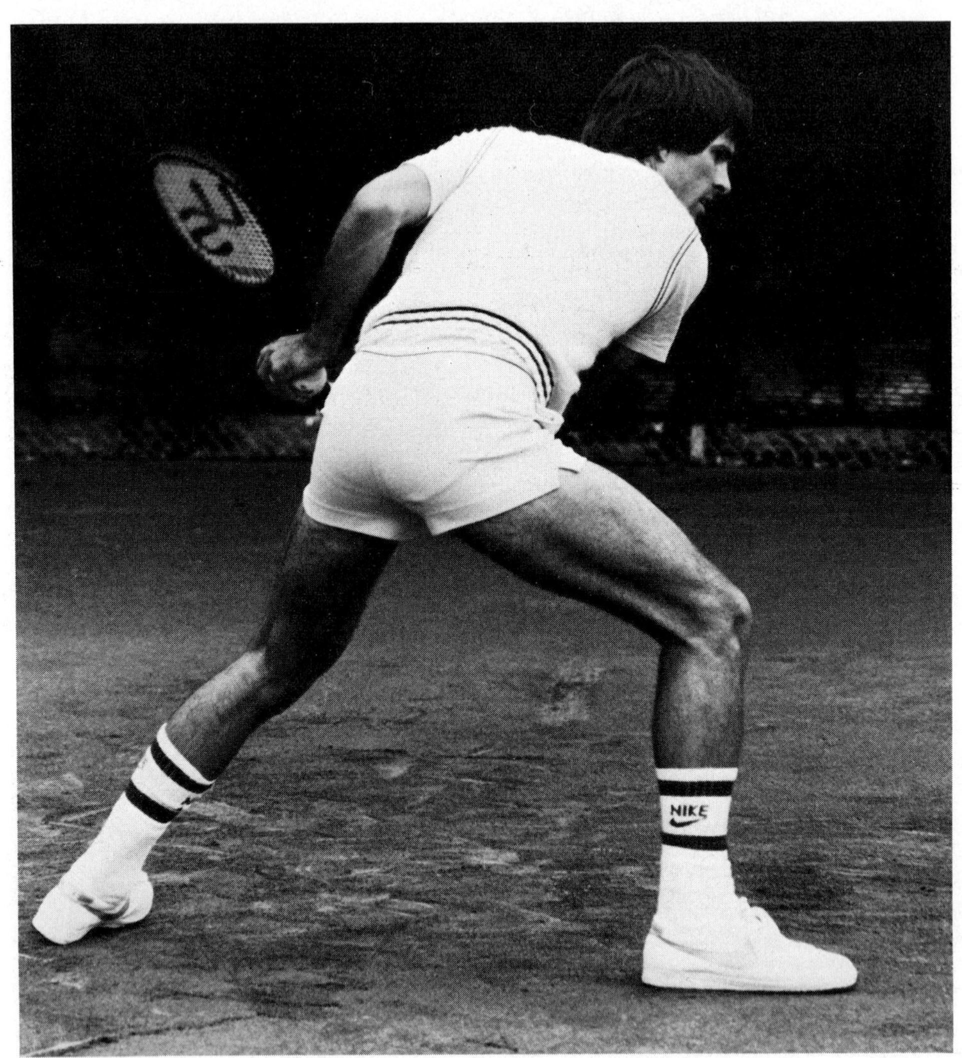

BUTCH WALTS/ranked in top 20

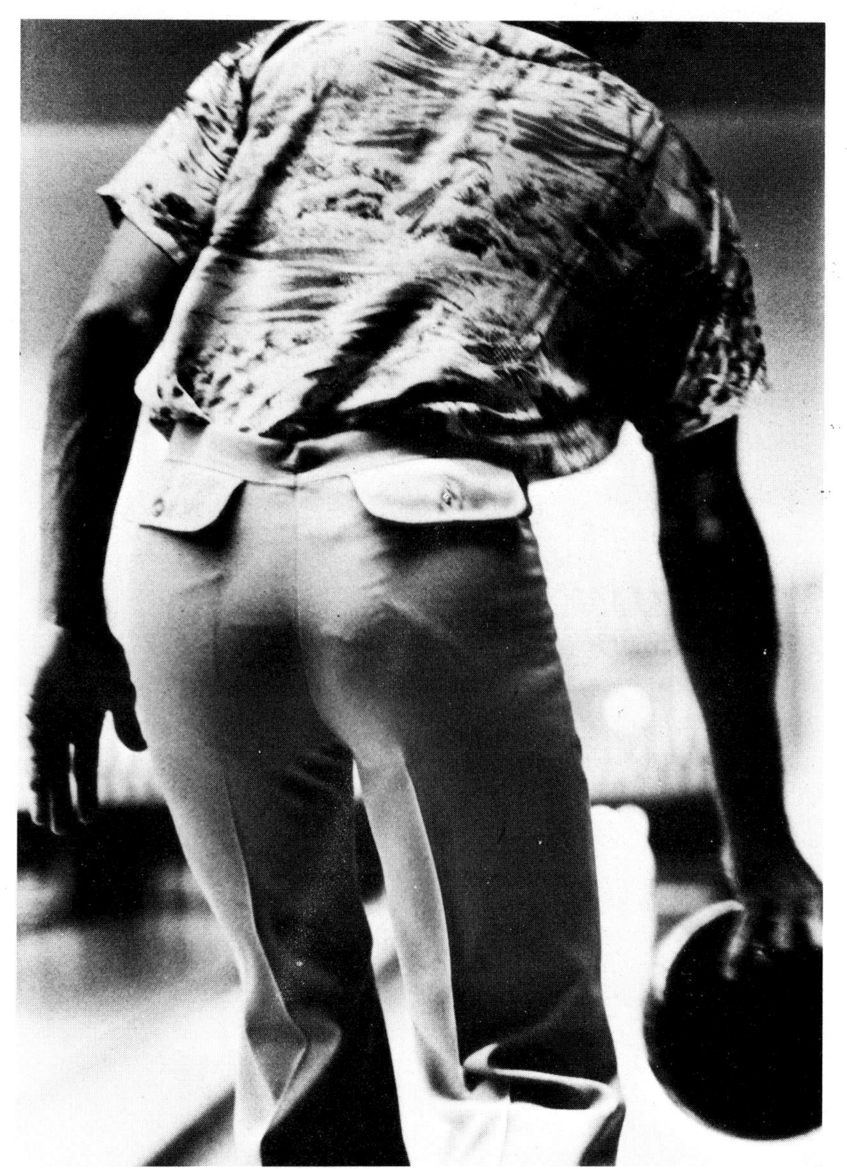

DUSTY

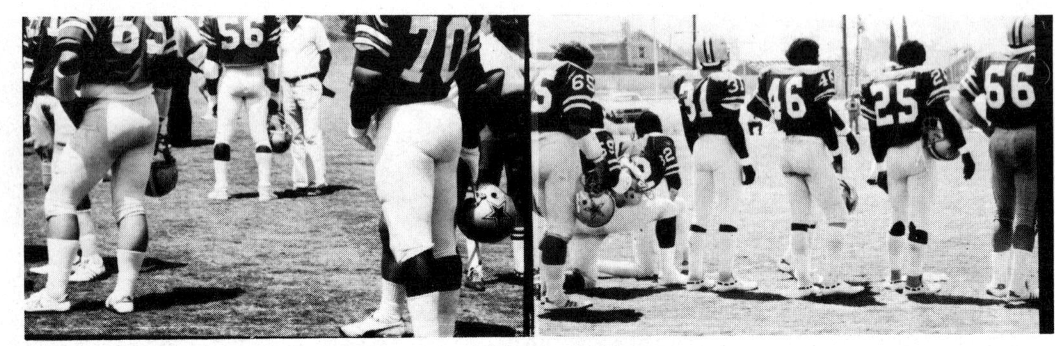

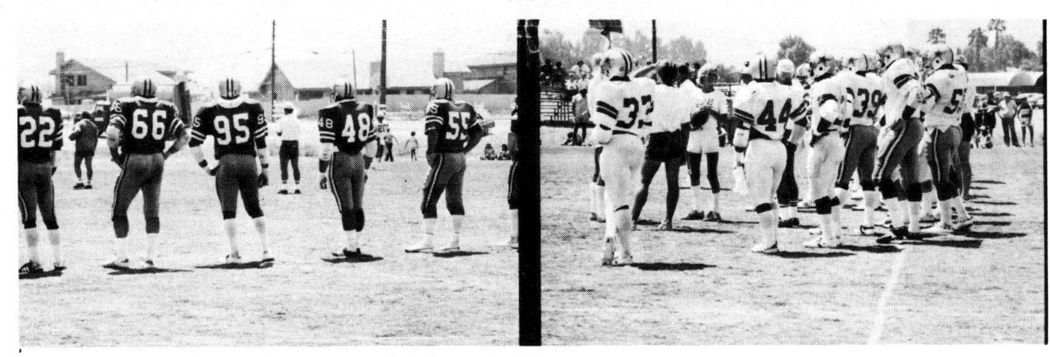

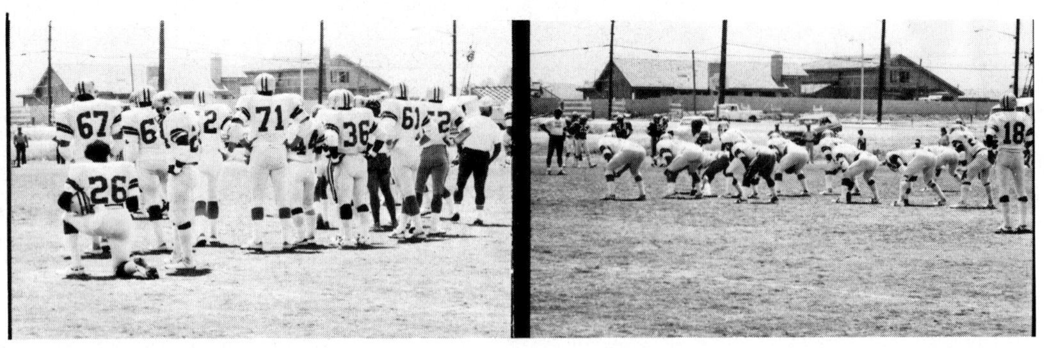

THE DALLAS COWBOYS

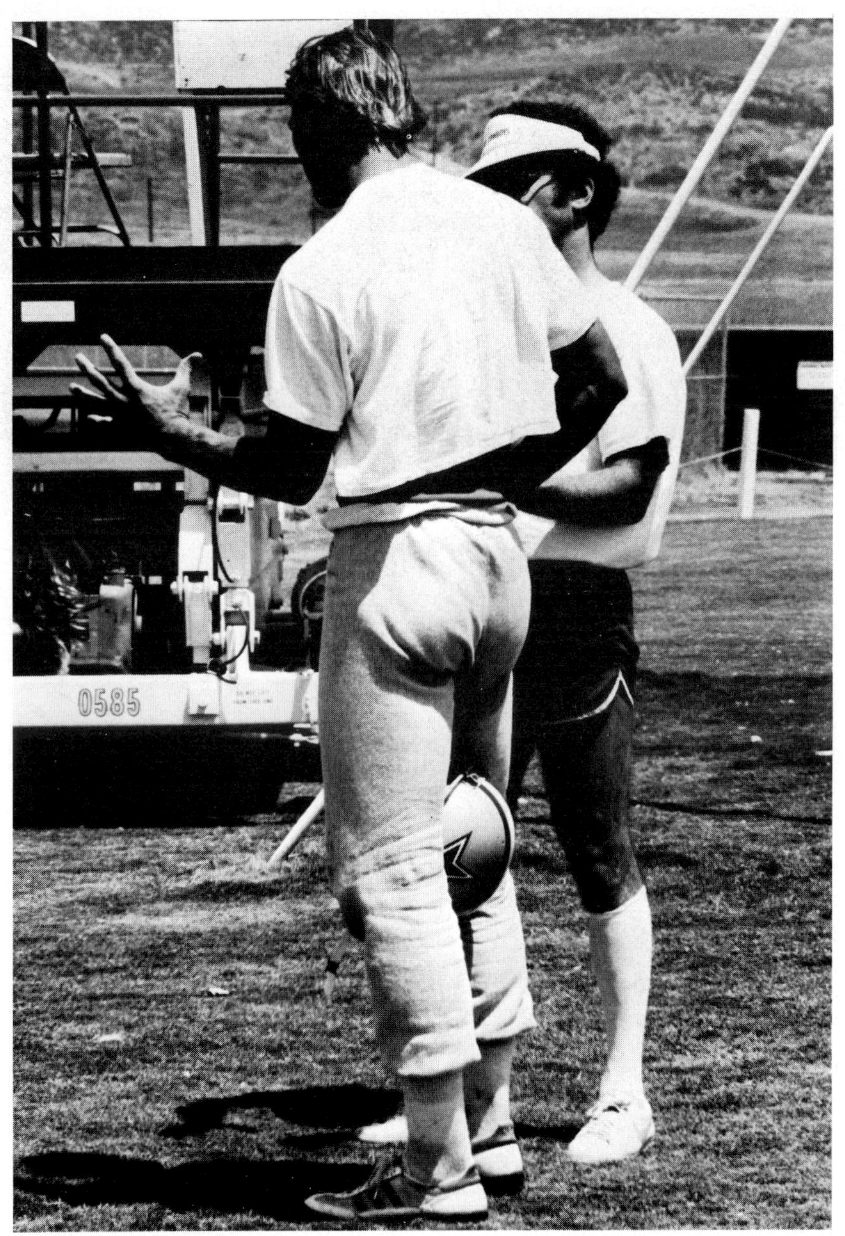

ROBERT STEELE

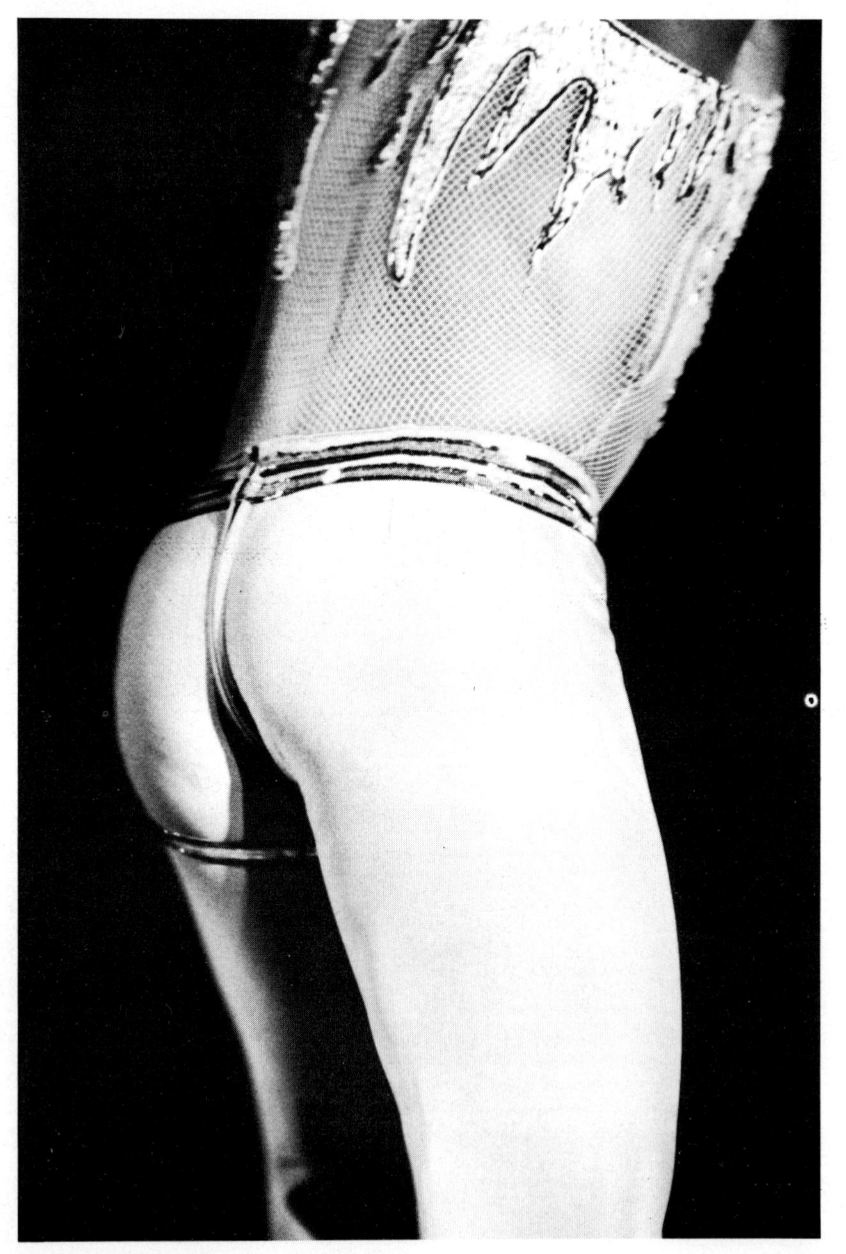

PAUL HEATH/Ice Follies

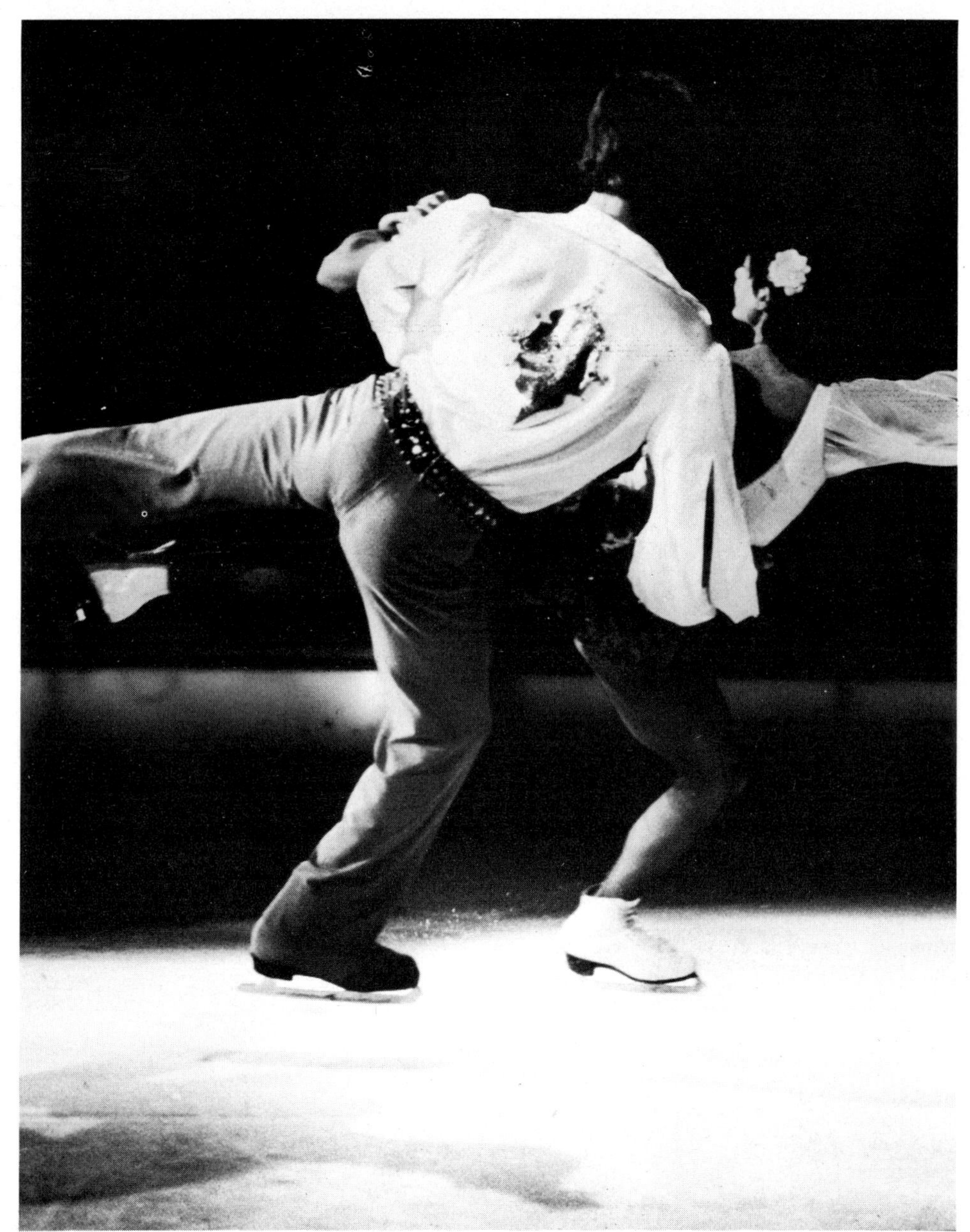

CHRIS HARRISON/
Ice Follies

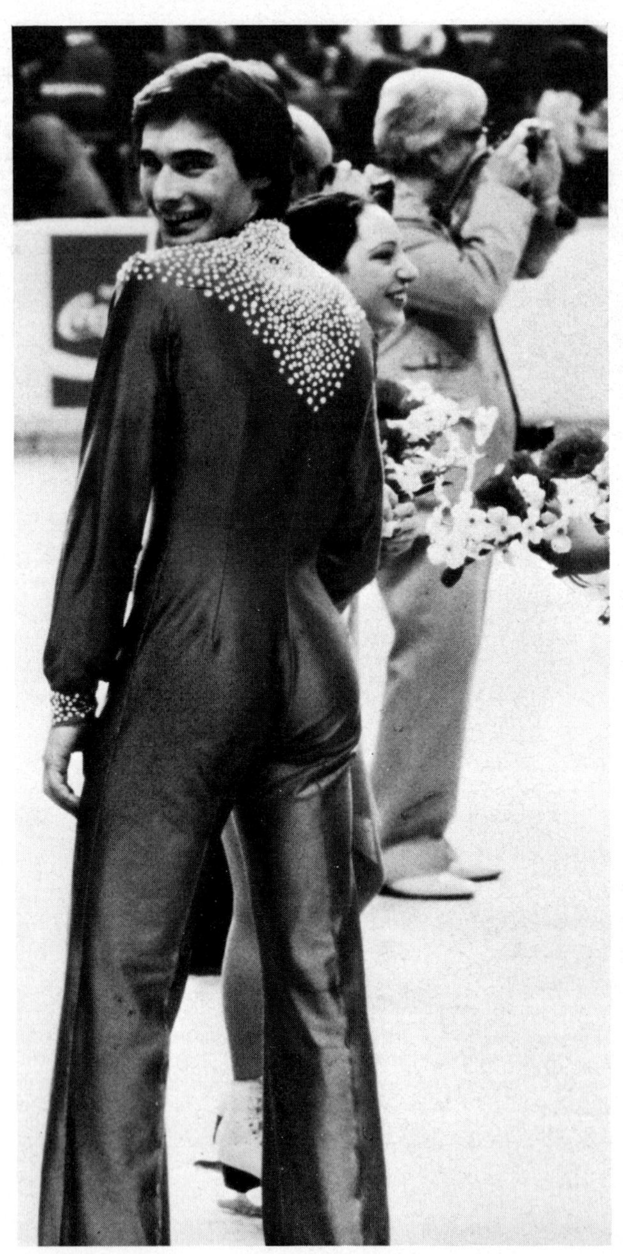

RANDY GARDNER/1979 World Champion Pairs Figure Skating/ 5 times National Champion

KEN JOHNSON/*Ice Follies*

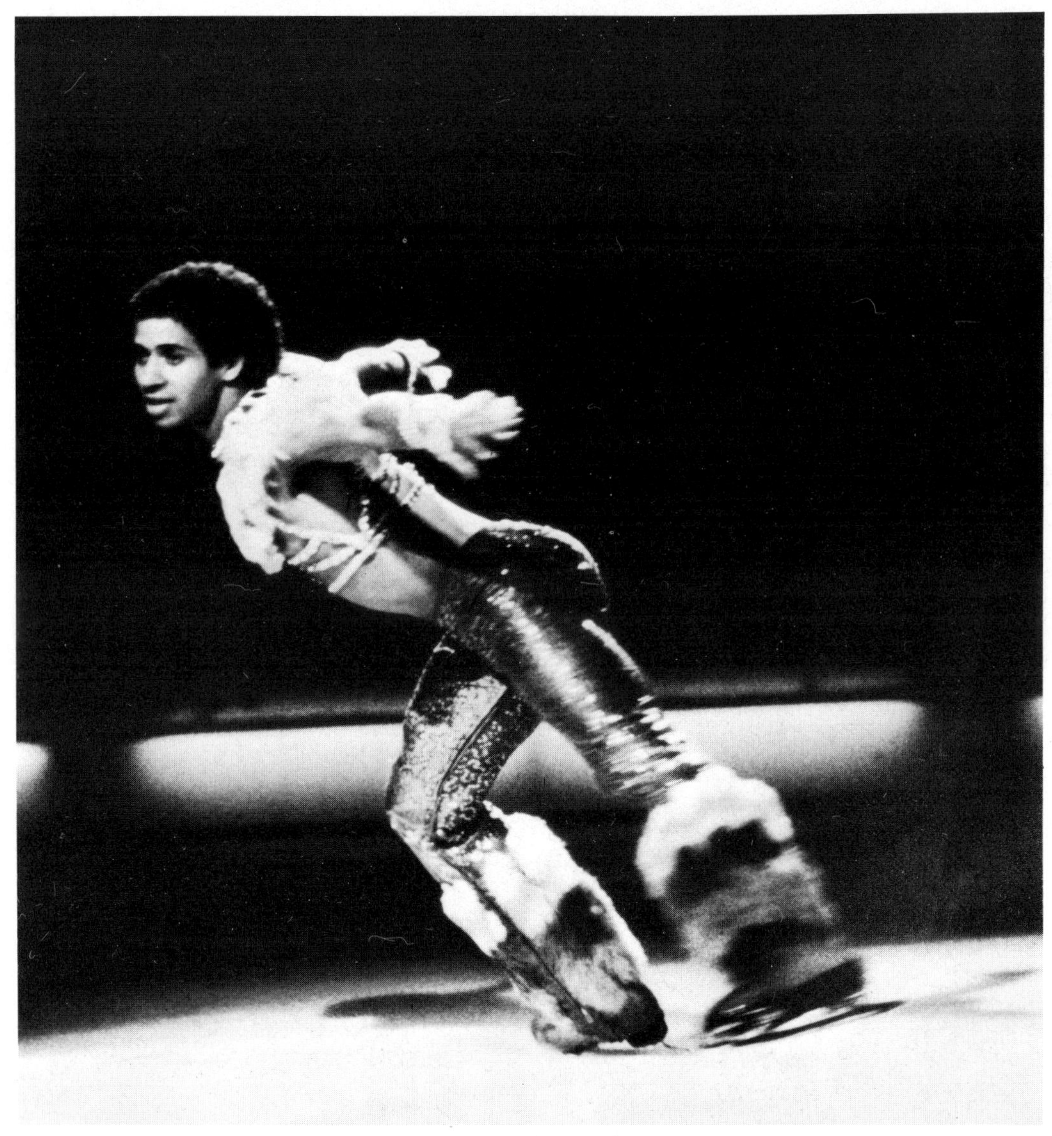

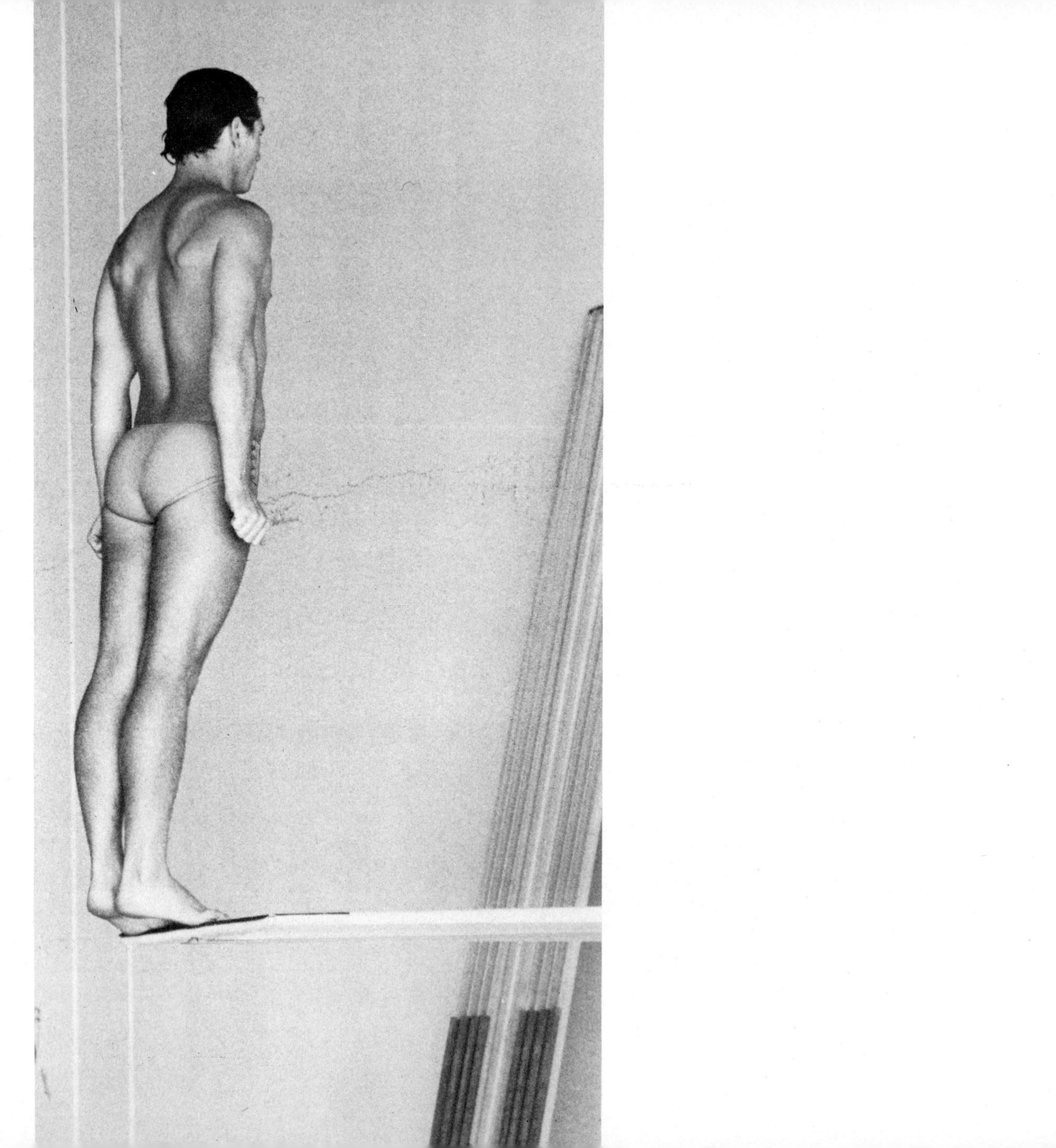

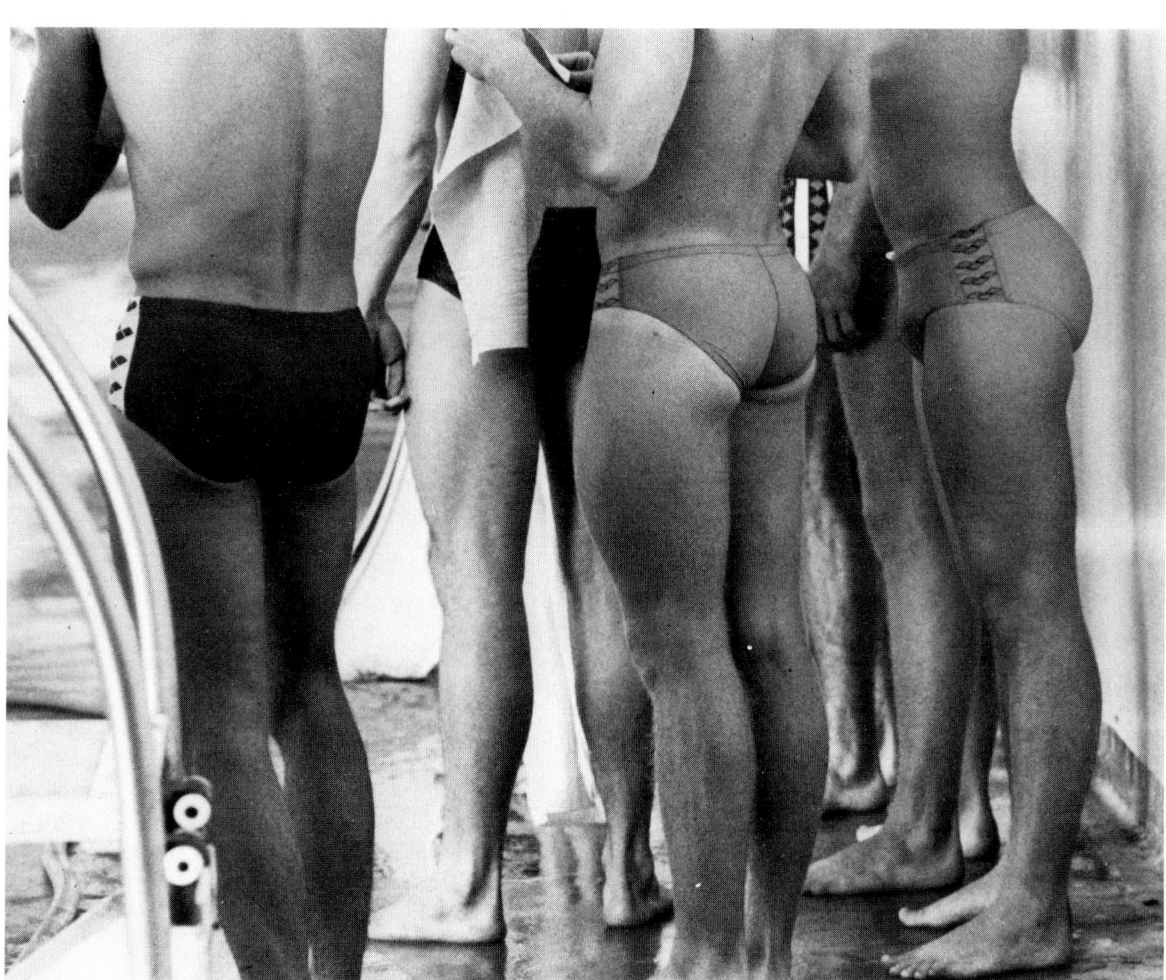

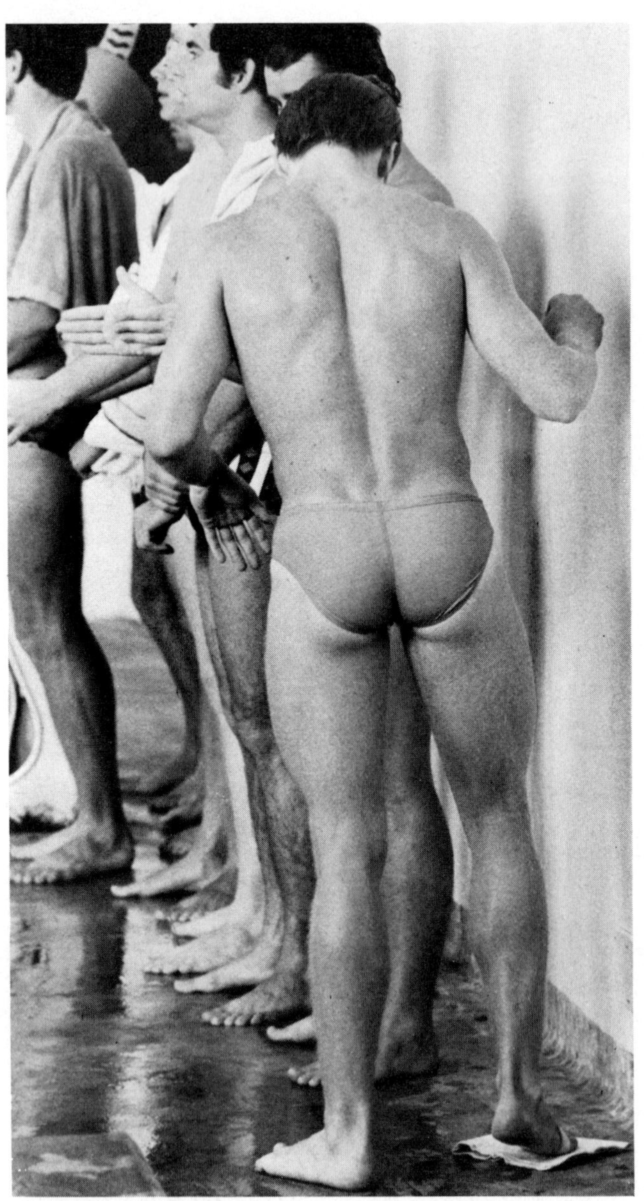

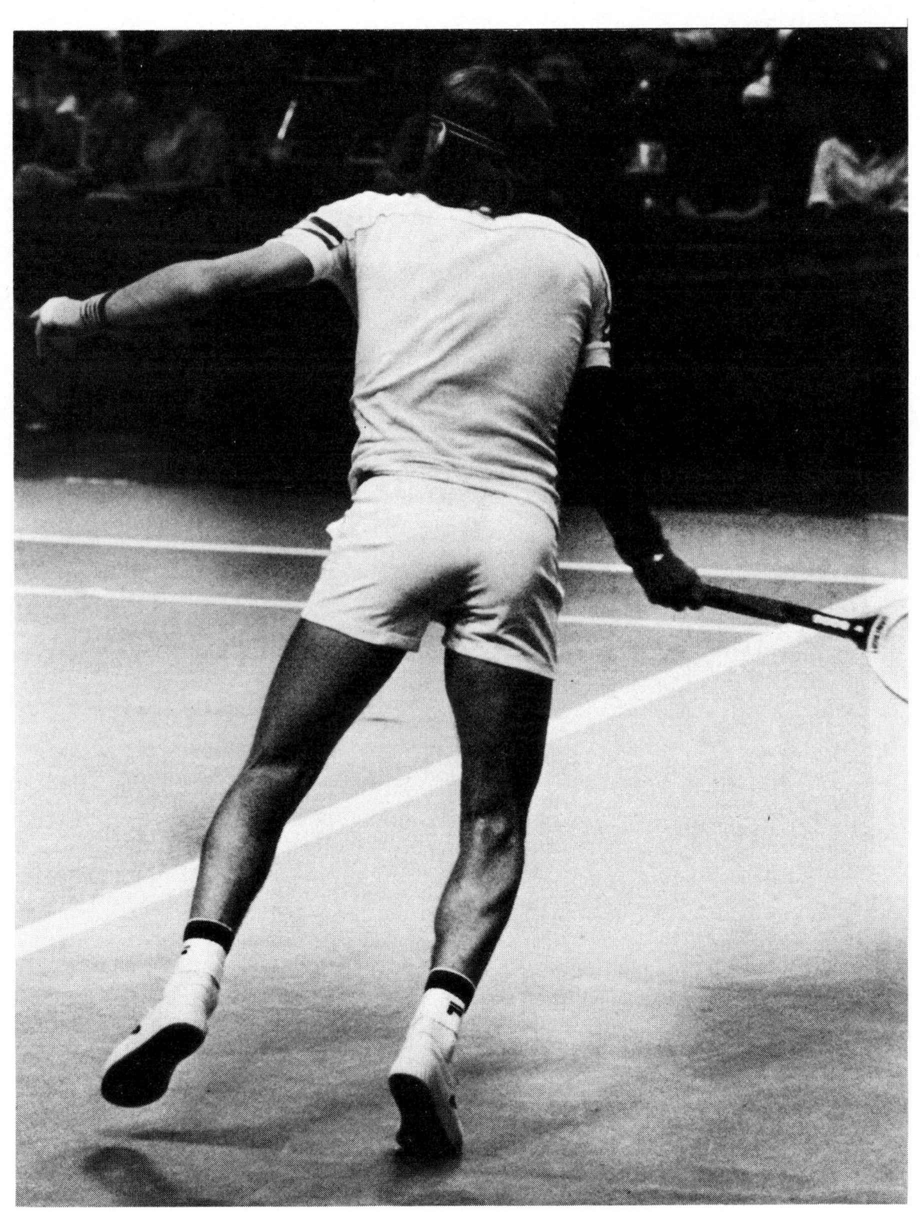

BJORN BORG

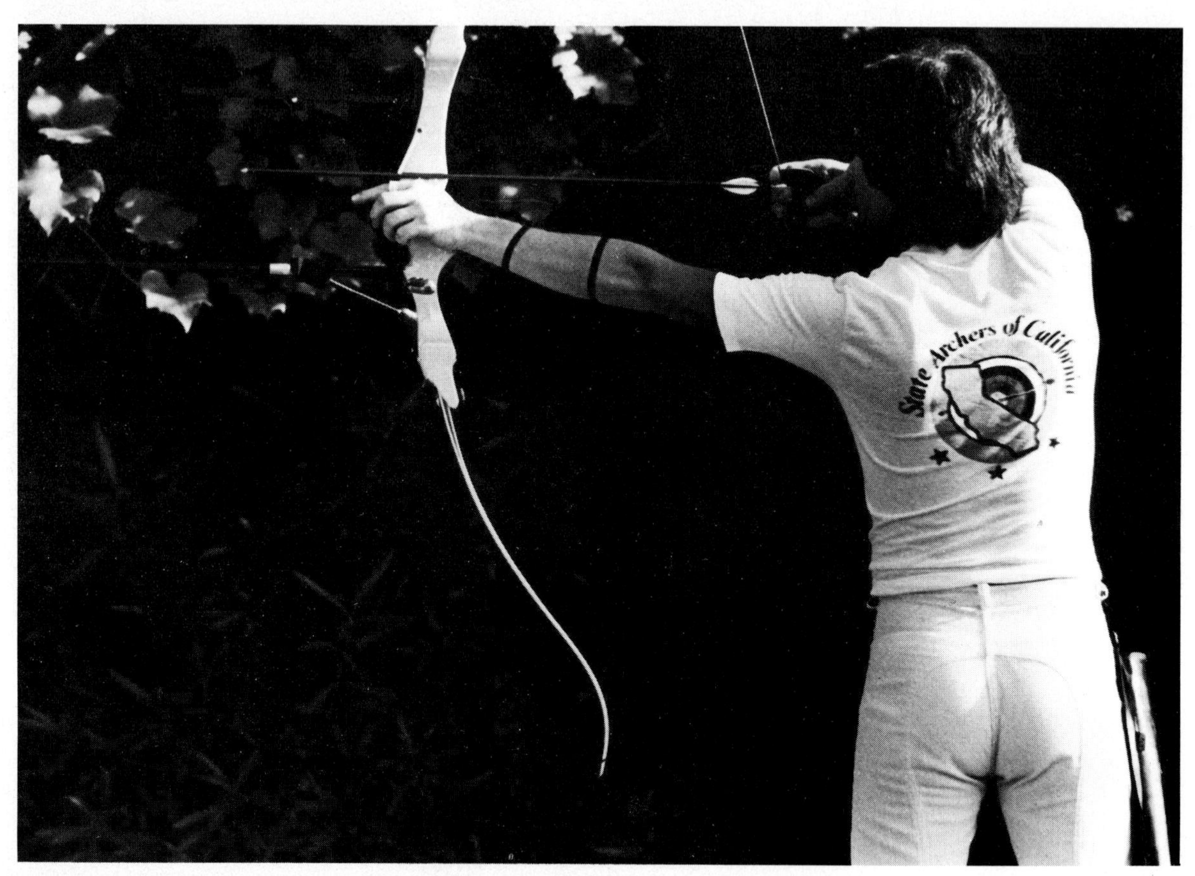

DON RABSKA/ranked in the nation's top ten

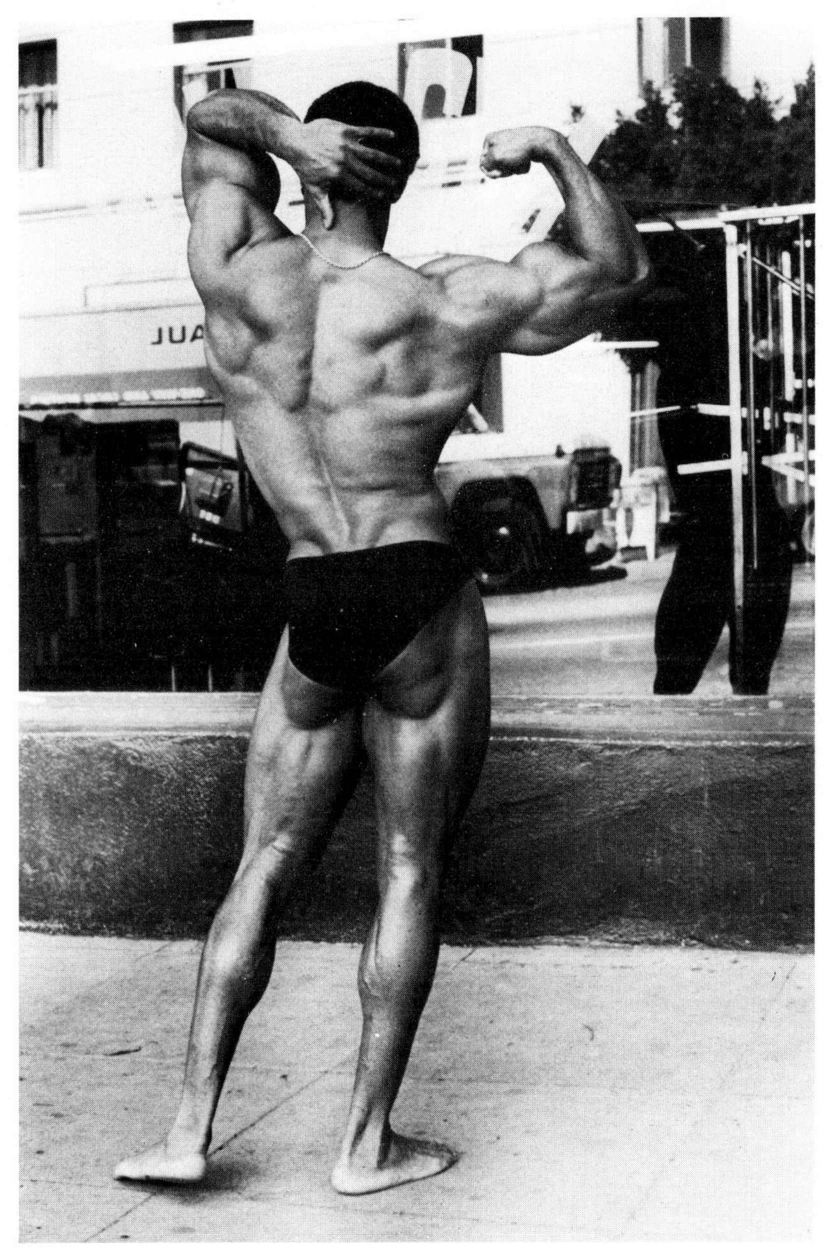

*BILL GRANT/Mr. World/
Mr. America*

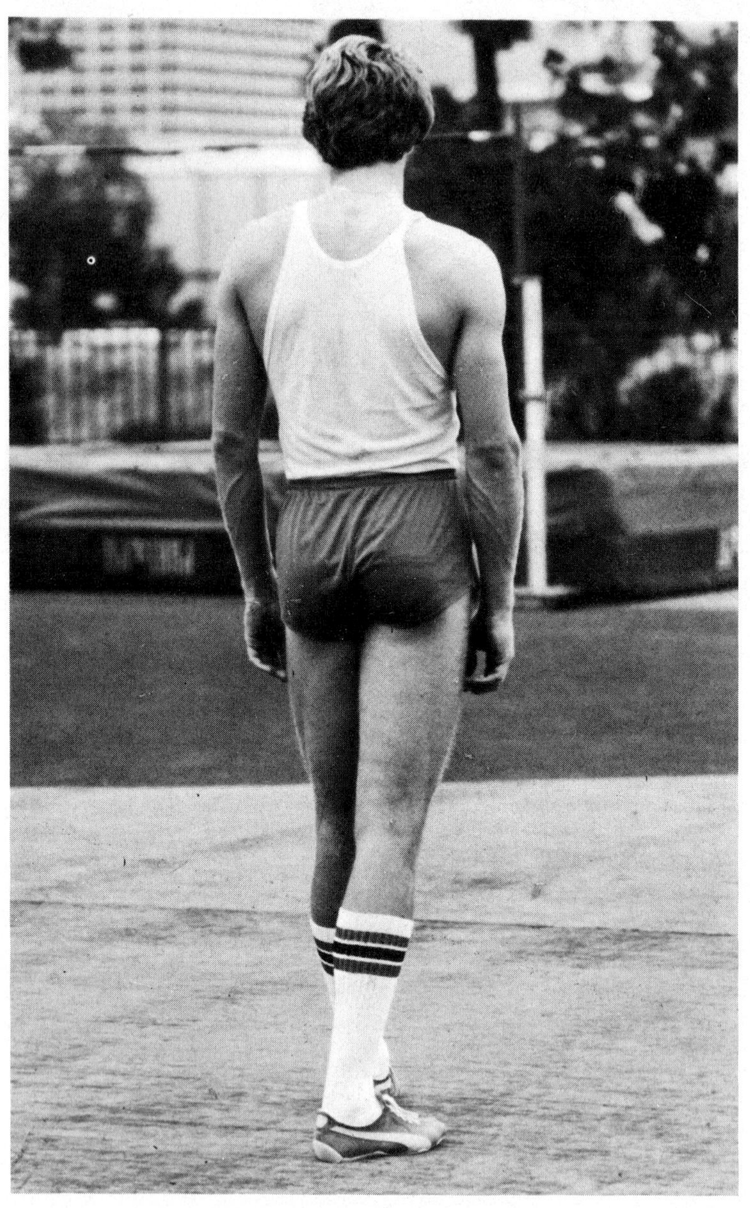

DWIGHT STONES/
10 times World Record holder, high jump/1972 and 1976 Olympic Bronze Medalist

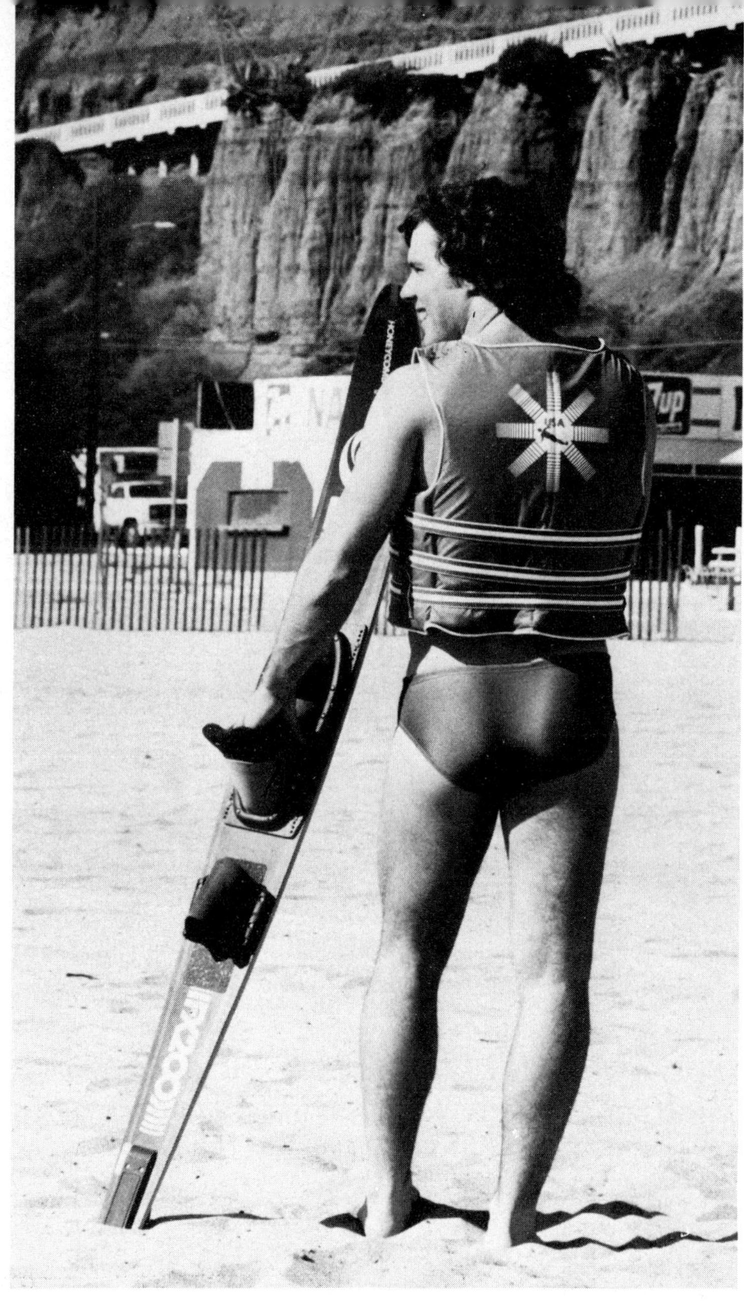

WAYNE GRIMDITCH/
16 times National Waterskiing Champion/3 times World Champion

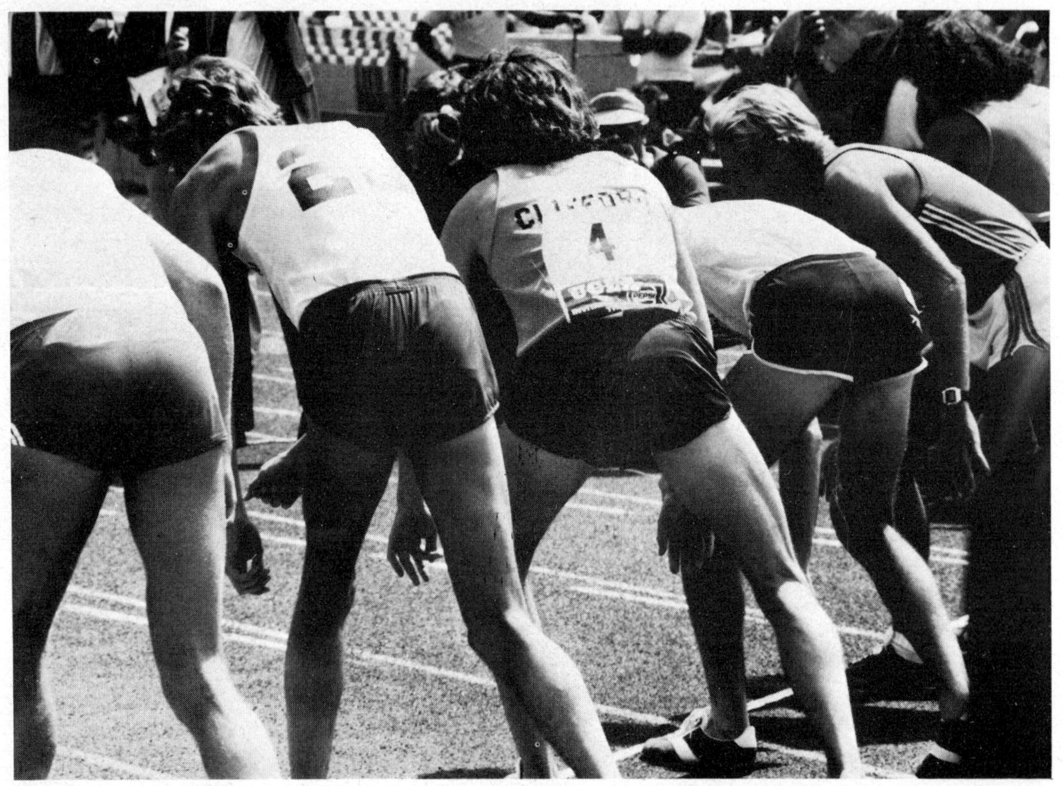

If you like looking at men's bodies in general, track meets are the best place to go. Everywhere you look, someone, somewhere on the field is stripping down and stretching out for the next event.

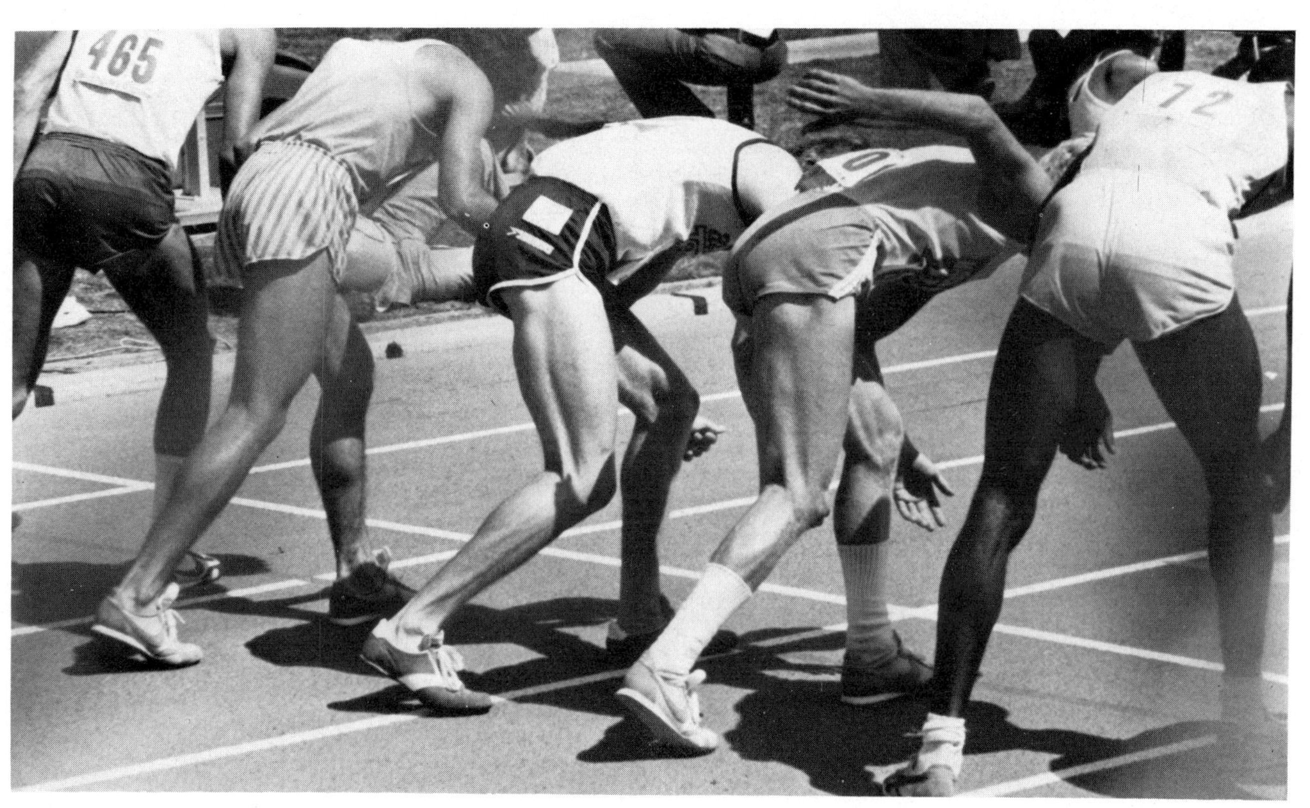
465
72

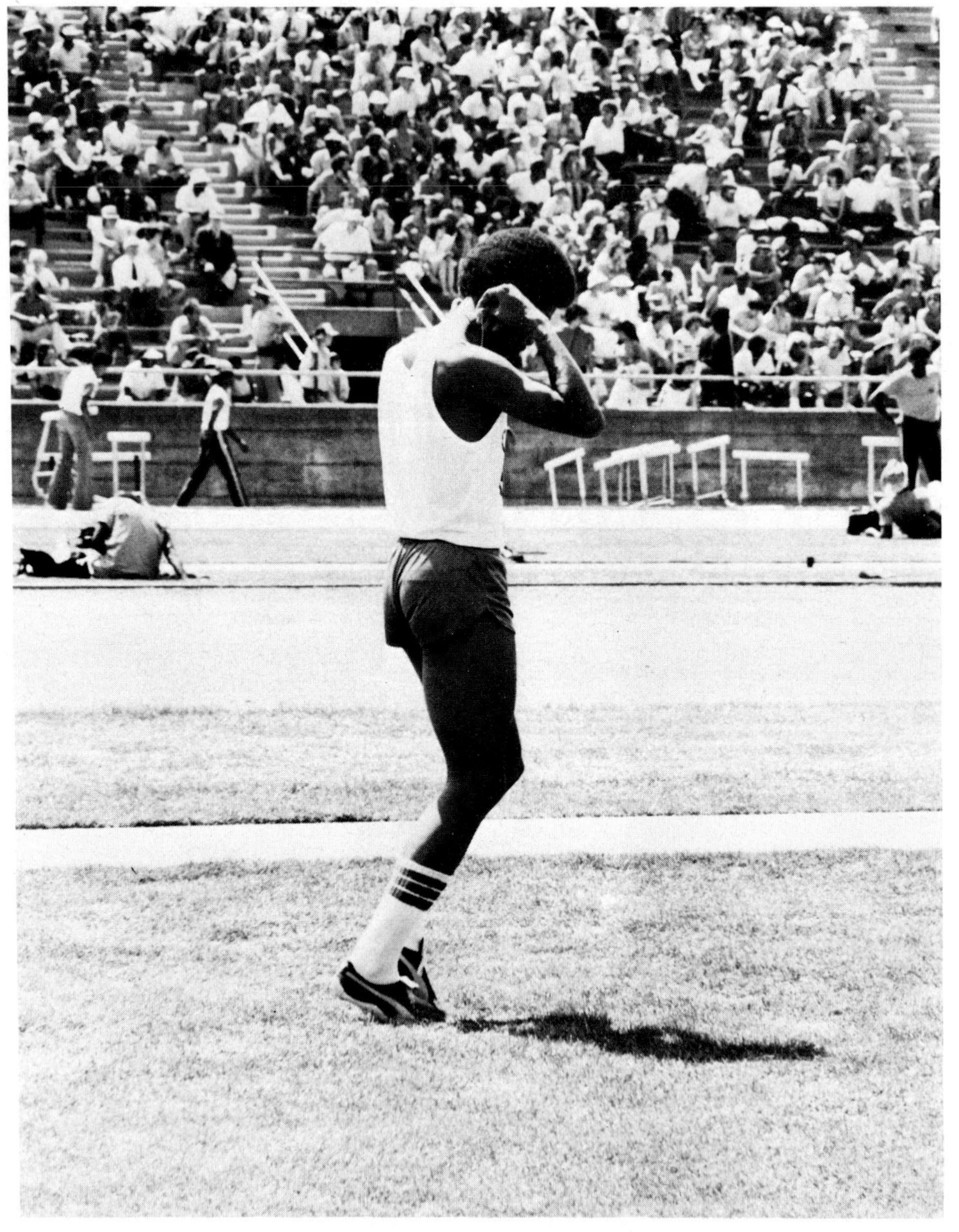

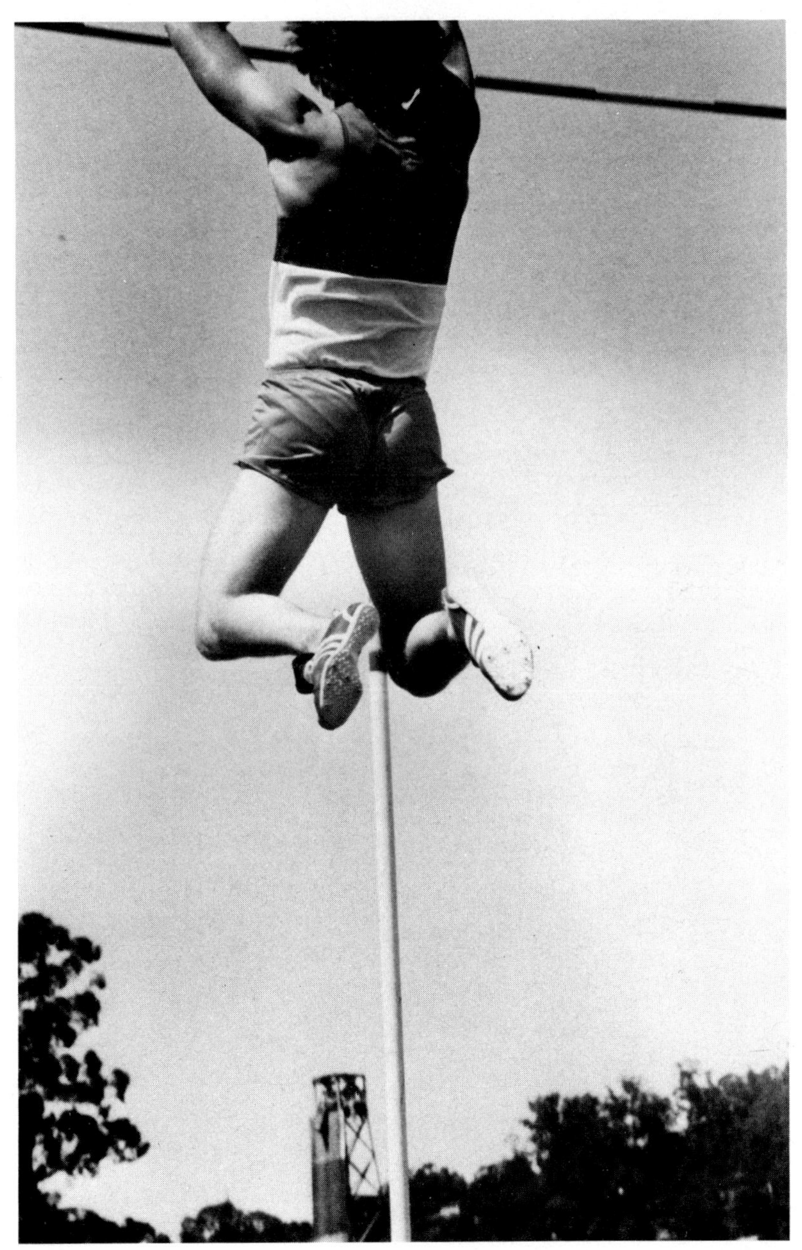

MIKE TULLY/ Former record holder/pole vault/2 time World Cup Champion

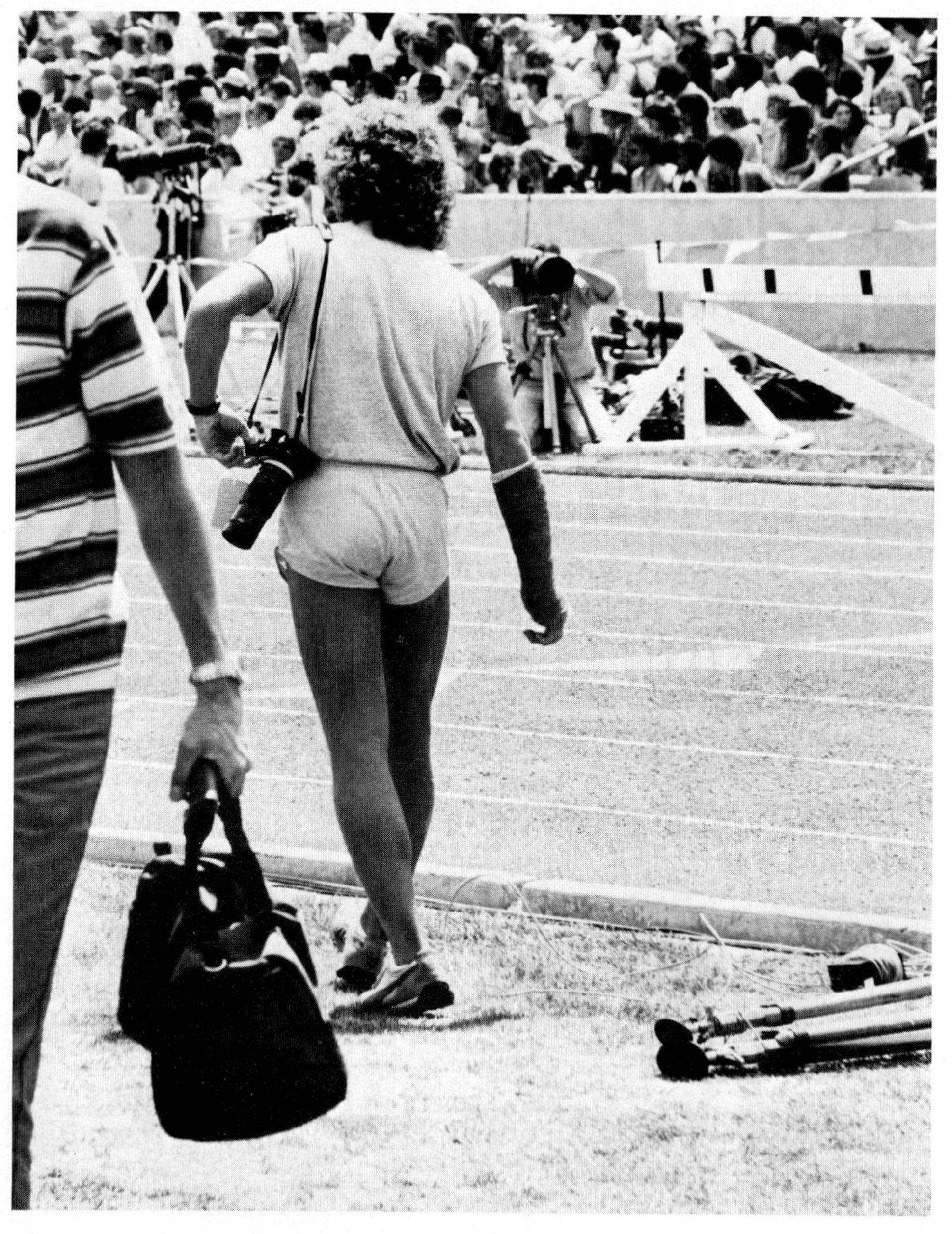

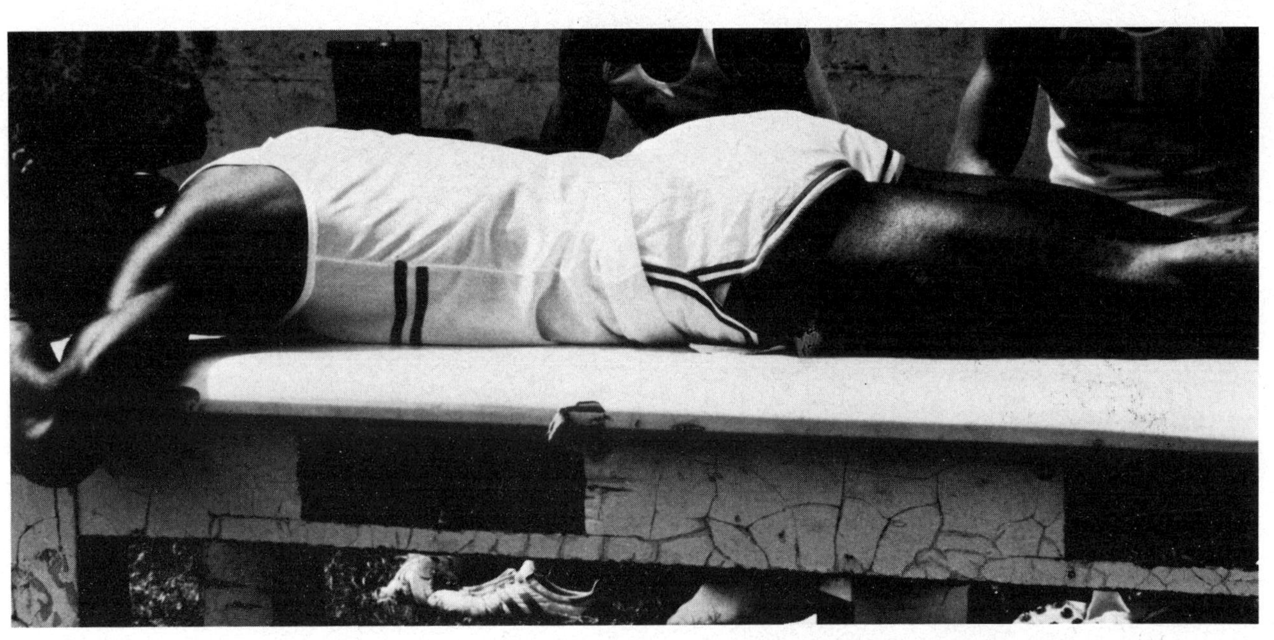

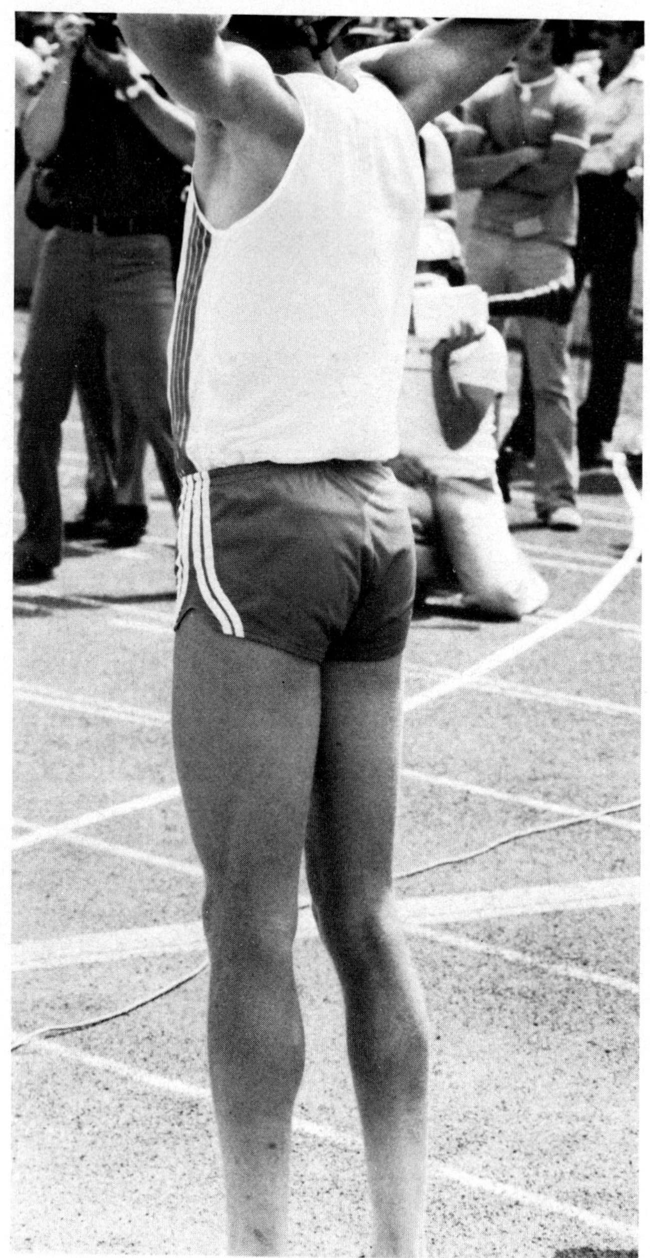

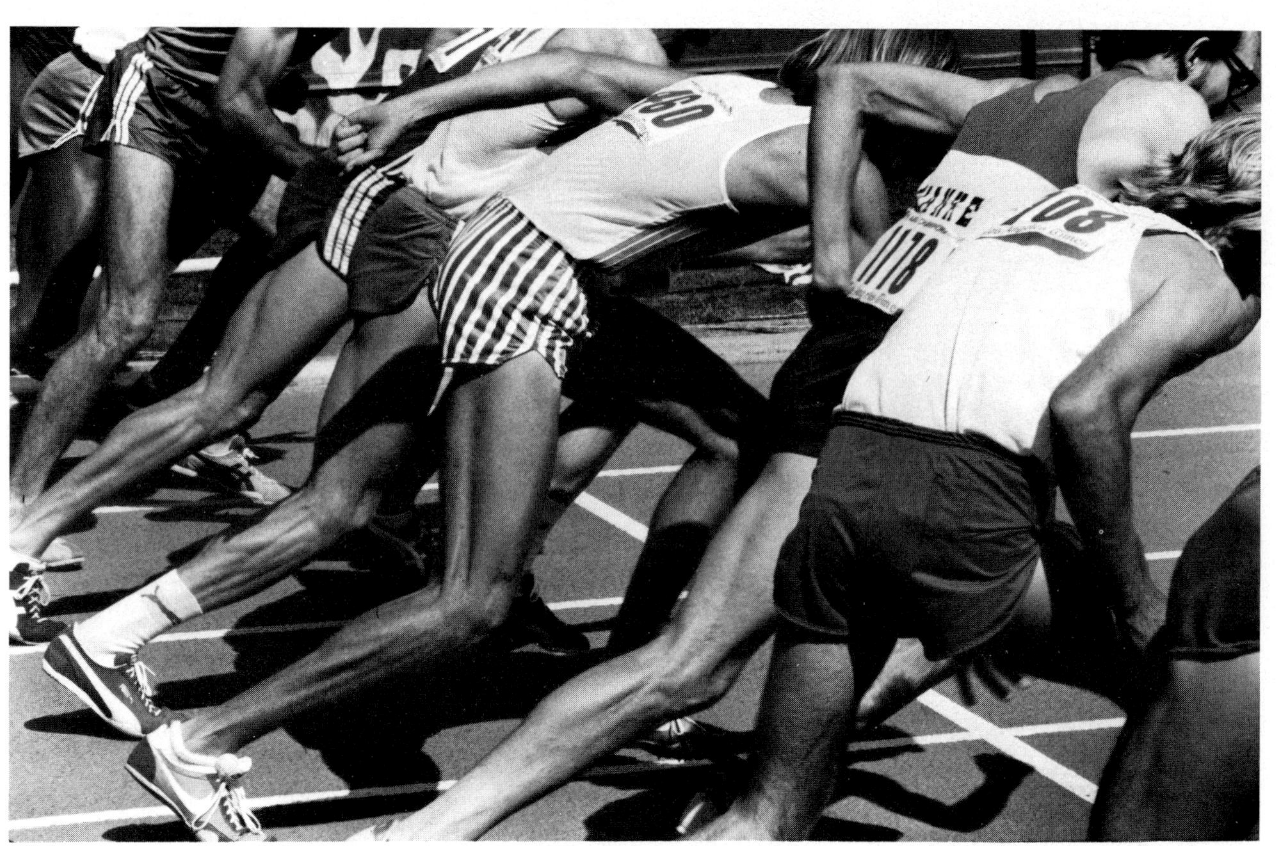

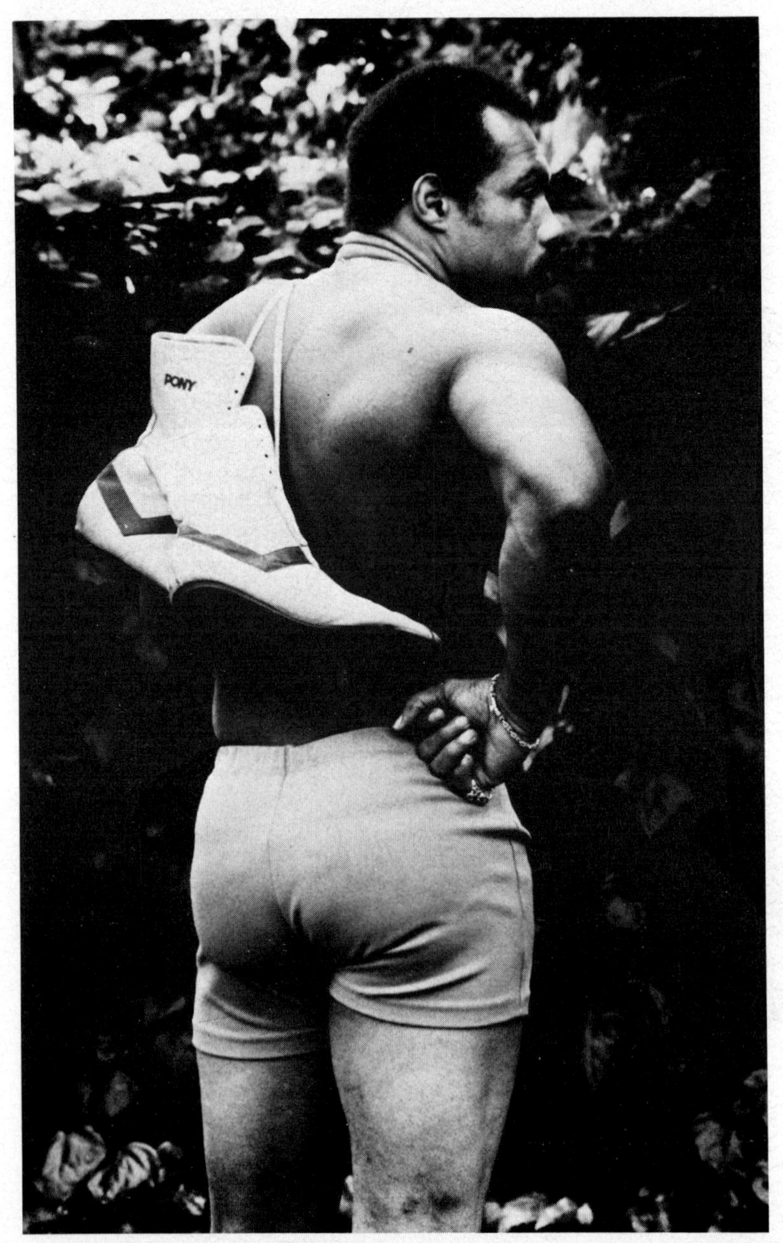

KEN NORTON/former WBC Heavyweight World Champion

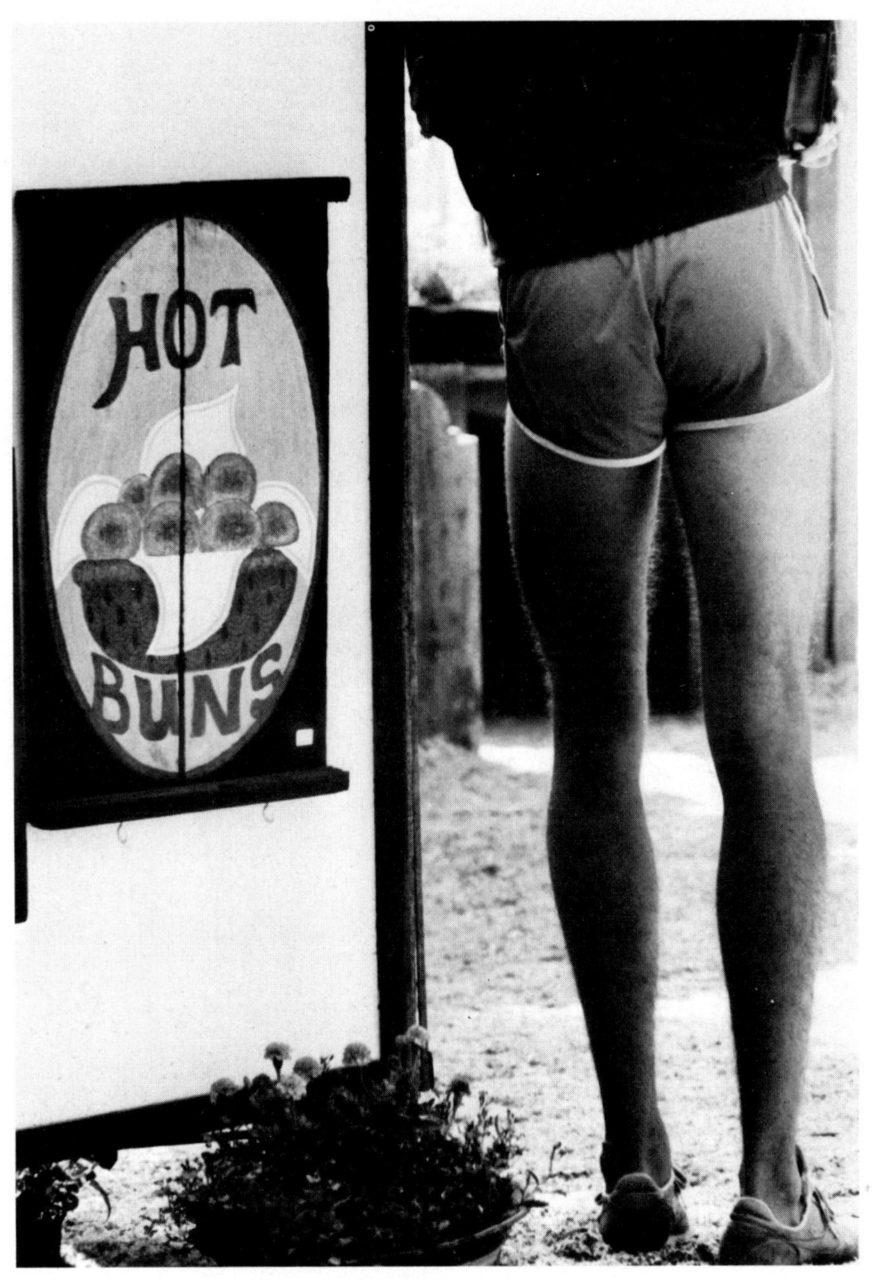

Arts-and-crafts show

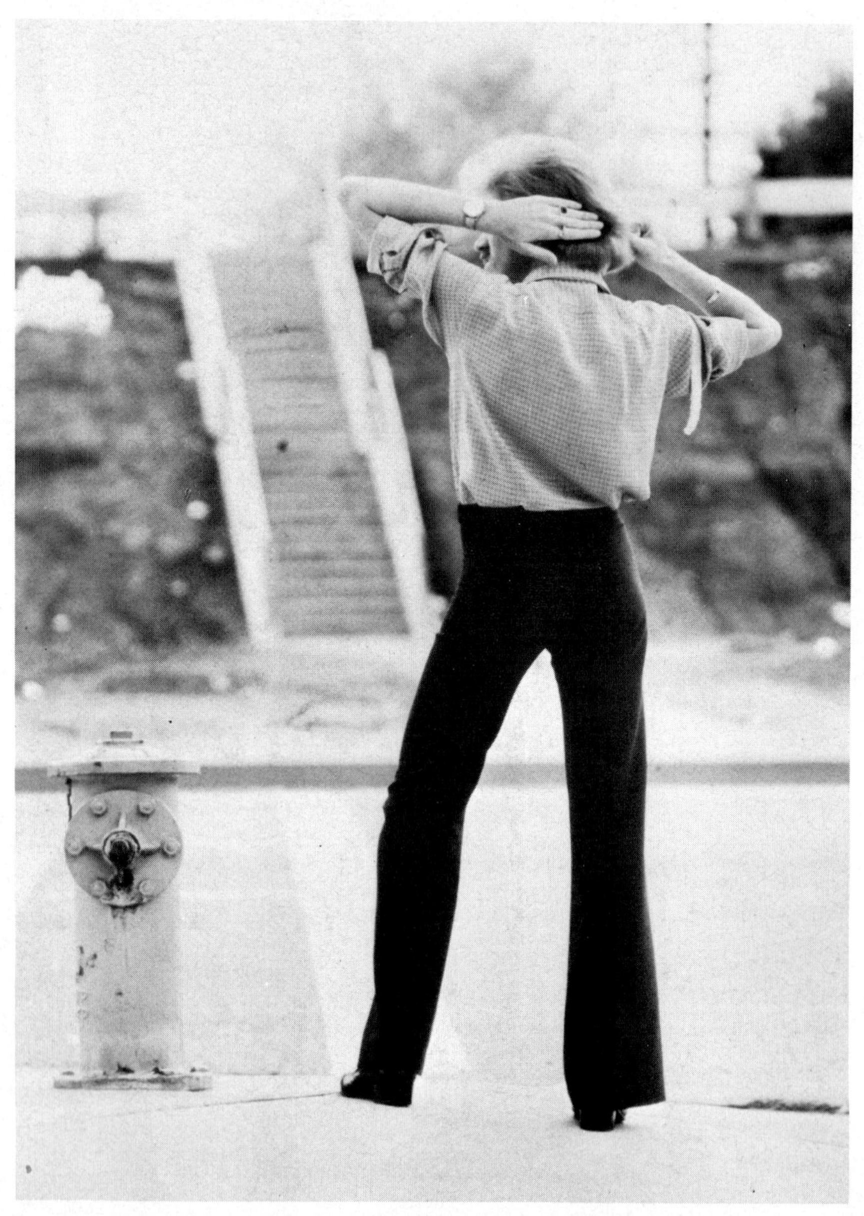

Santa Monica Boulevard

In the park

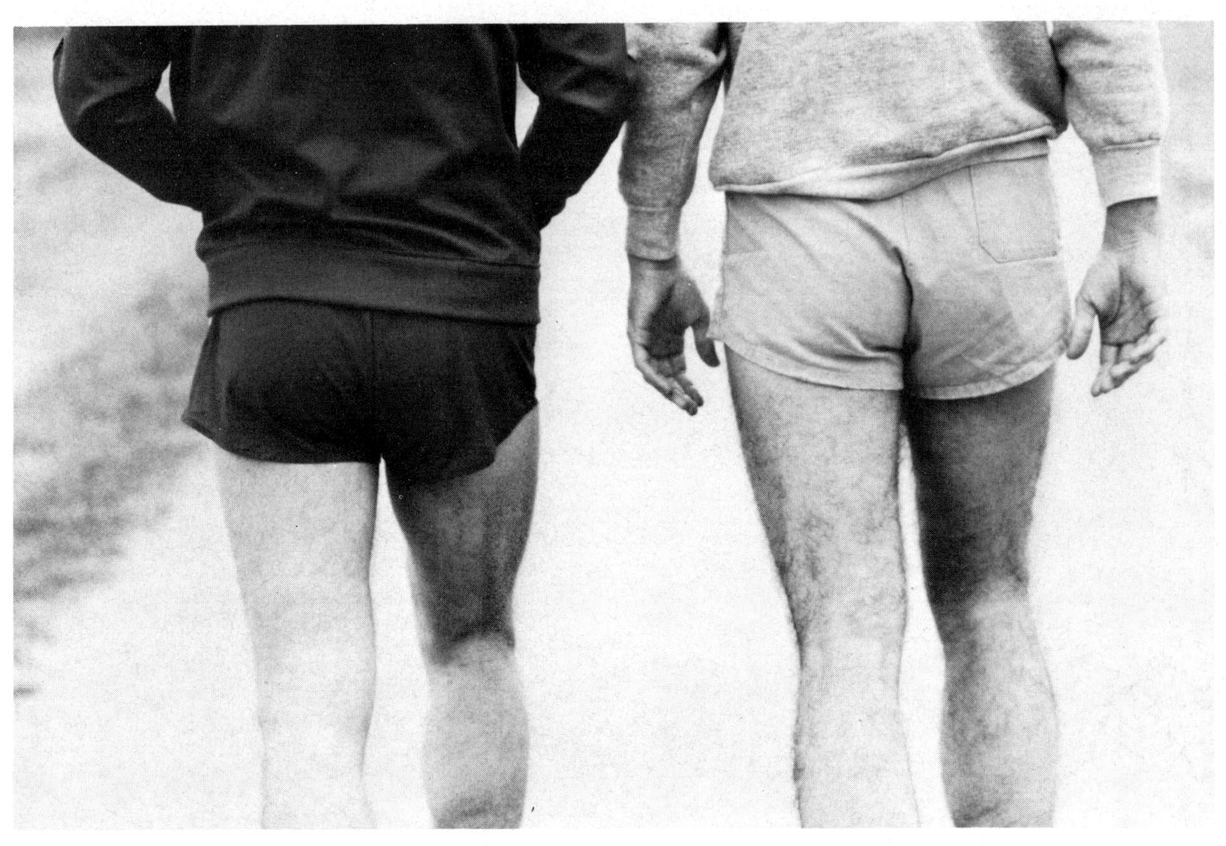

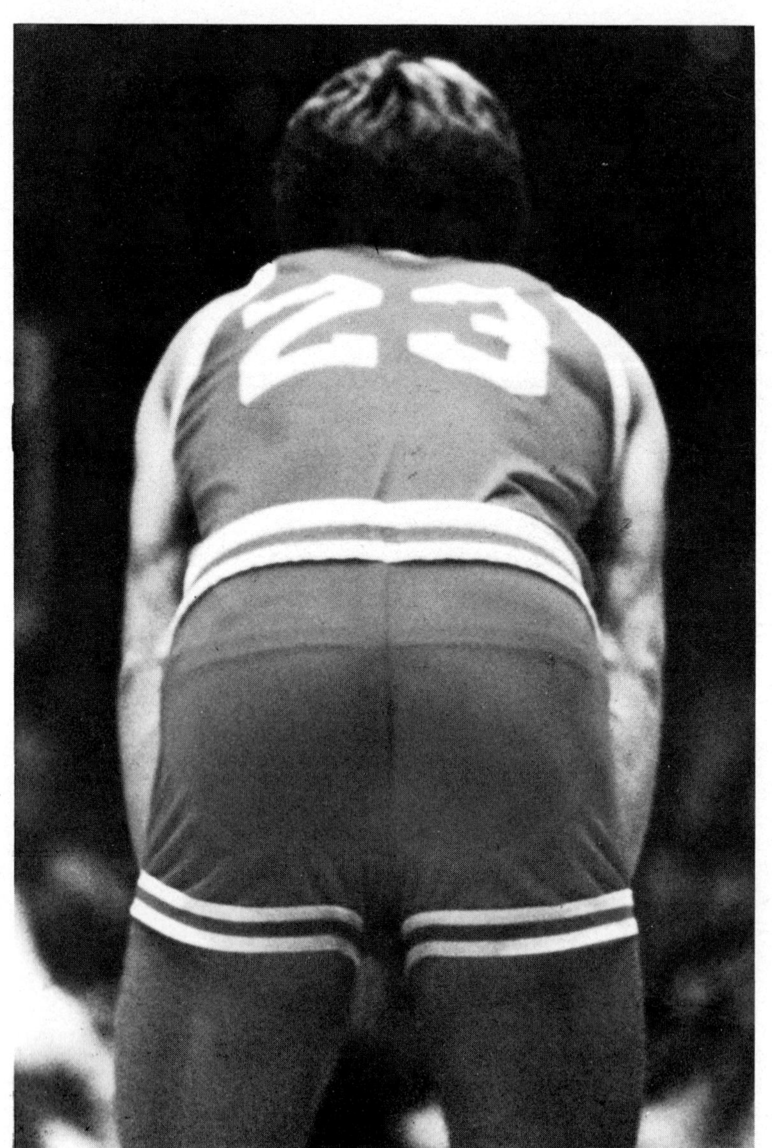
23

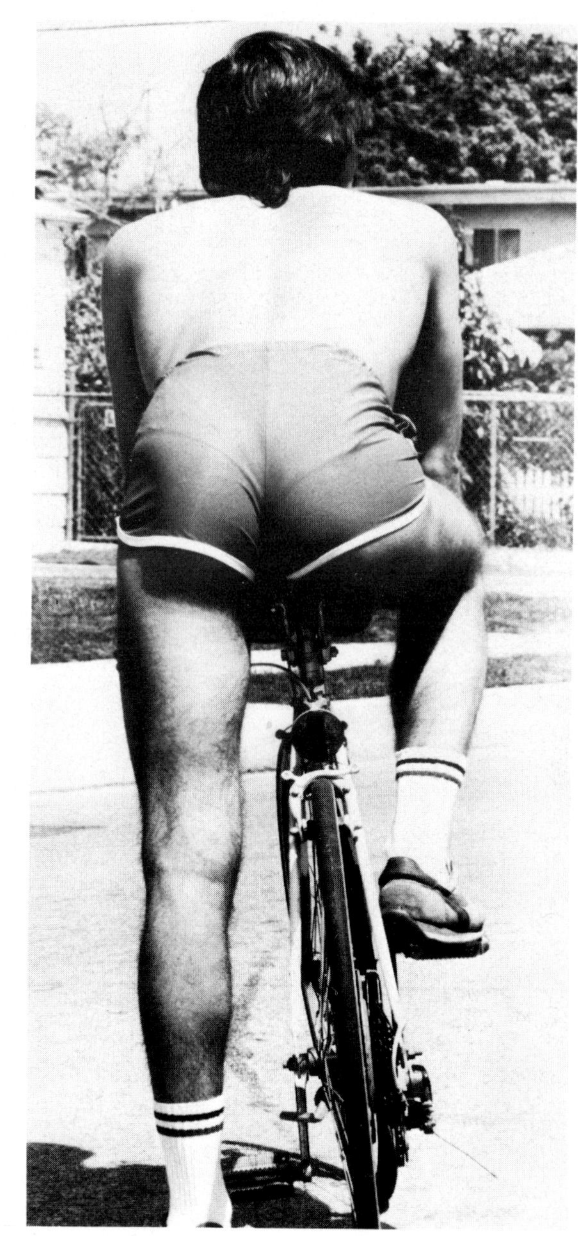

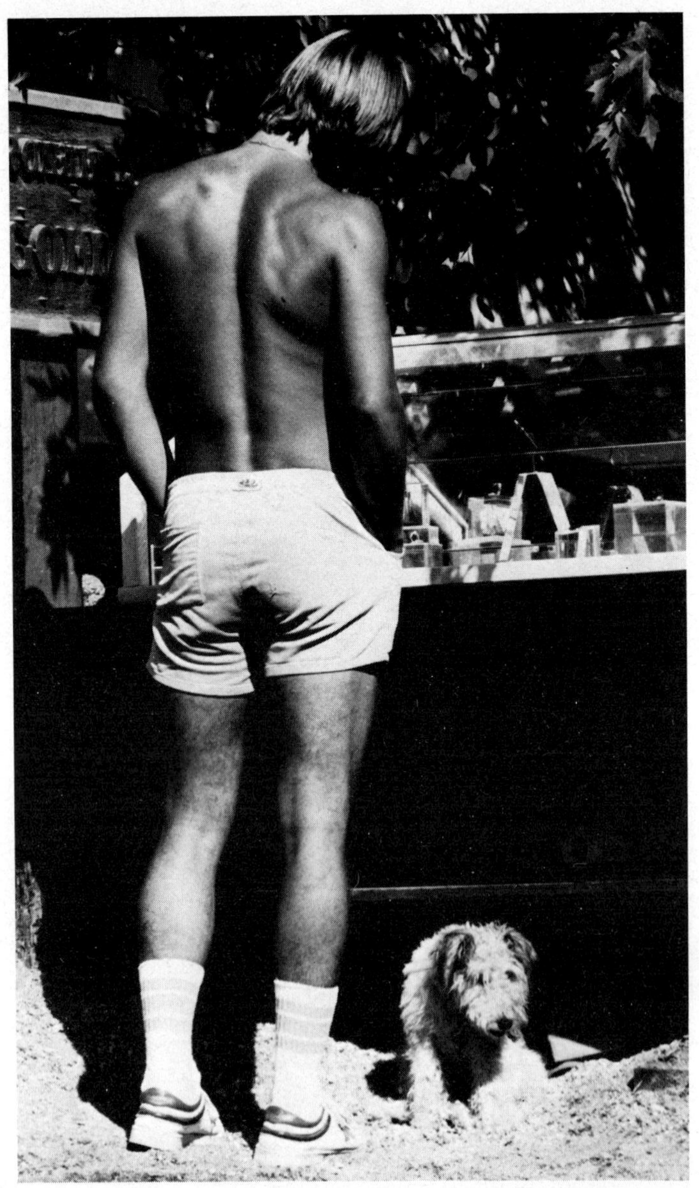

Arts-and-crafts festival

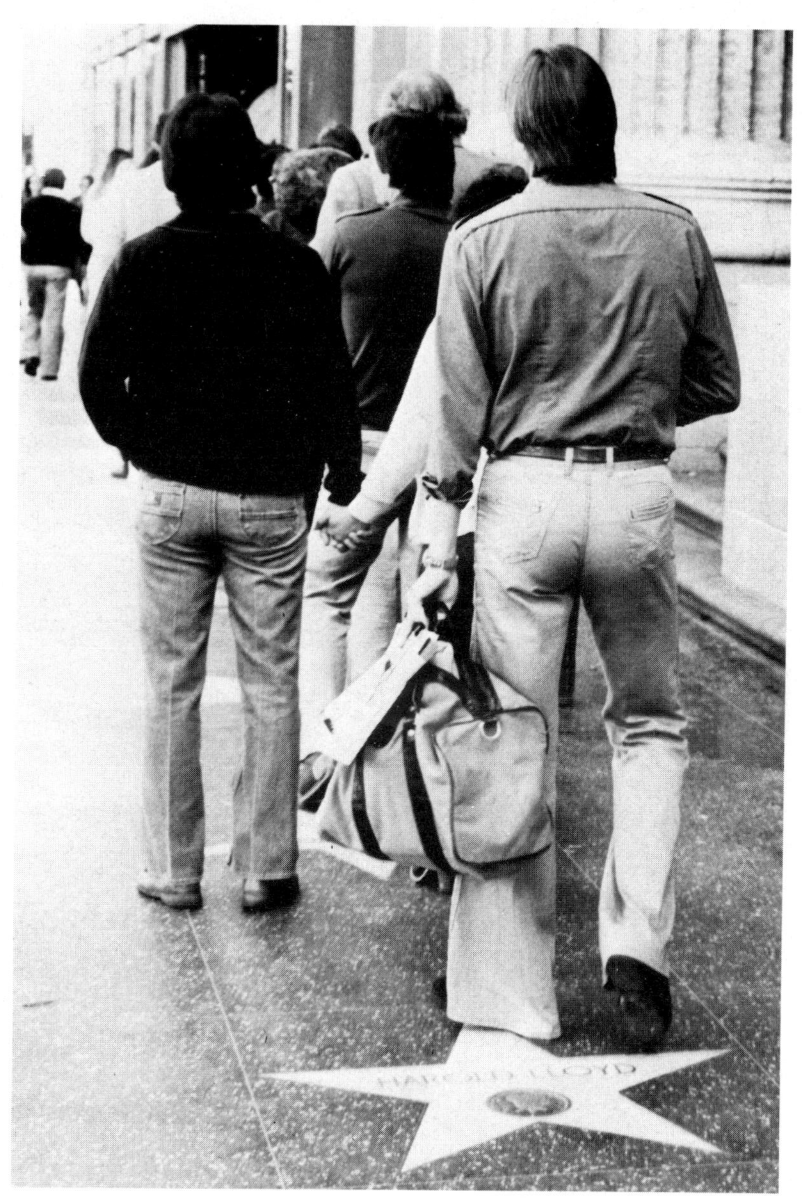

Hollywood Boulevard

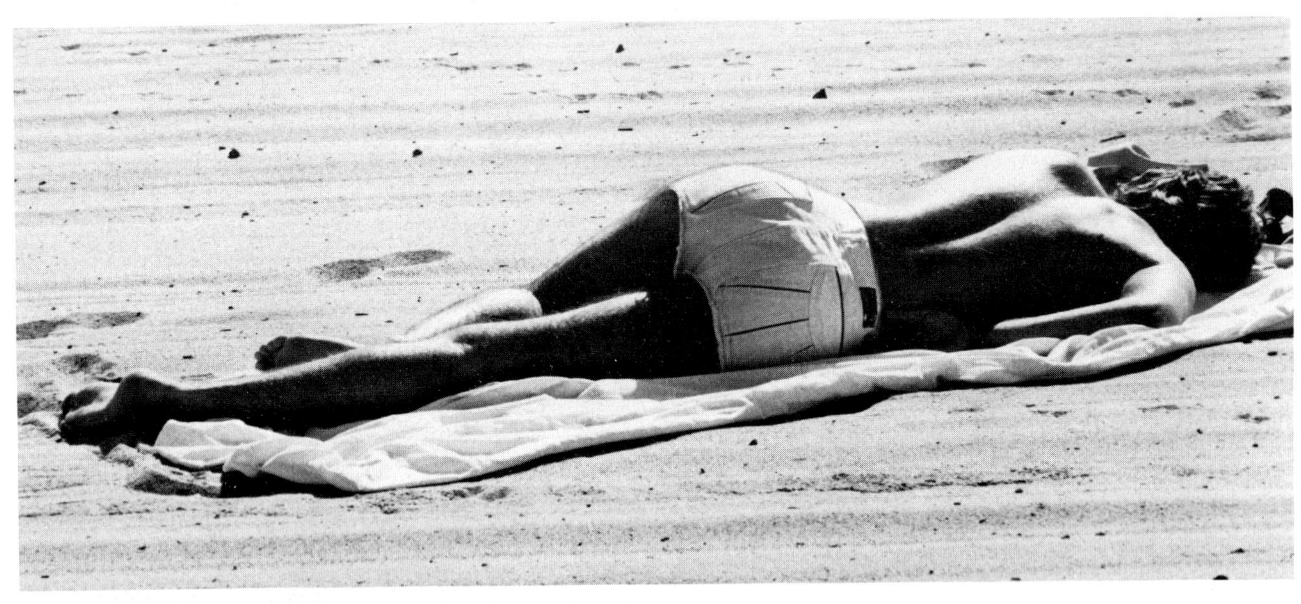

The beach

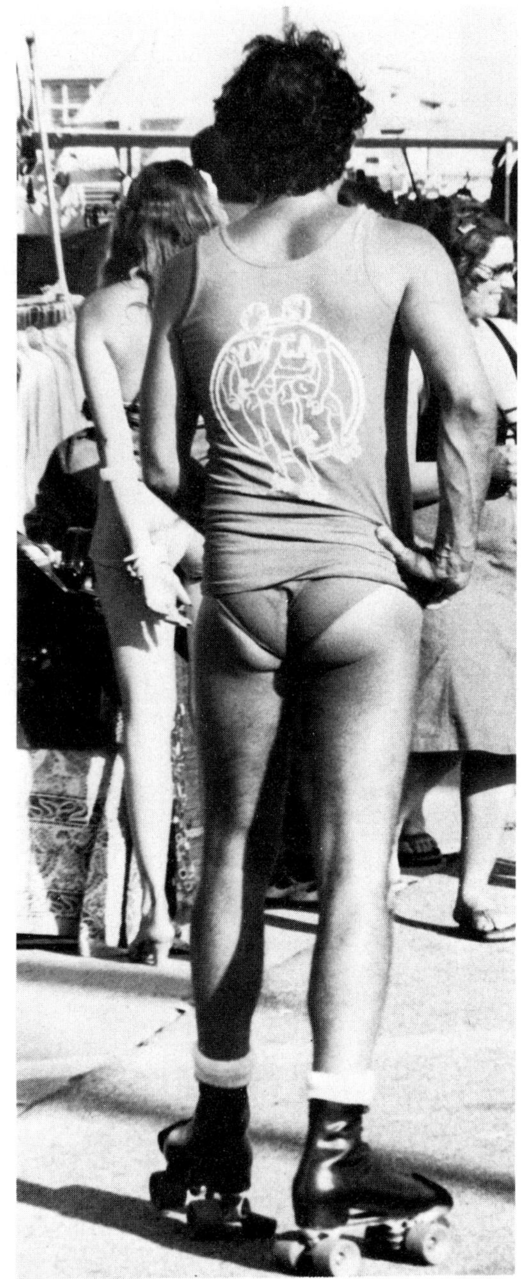

Roller skating in Venice: the newest Californian excuse for not getting dressed

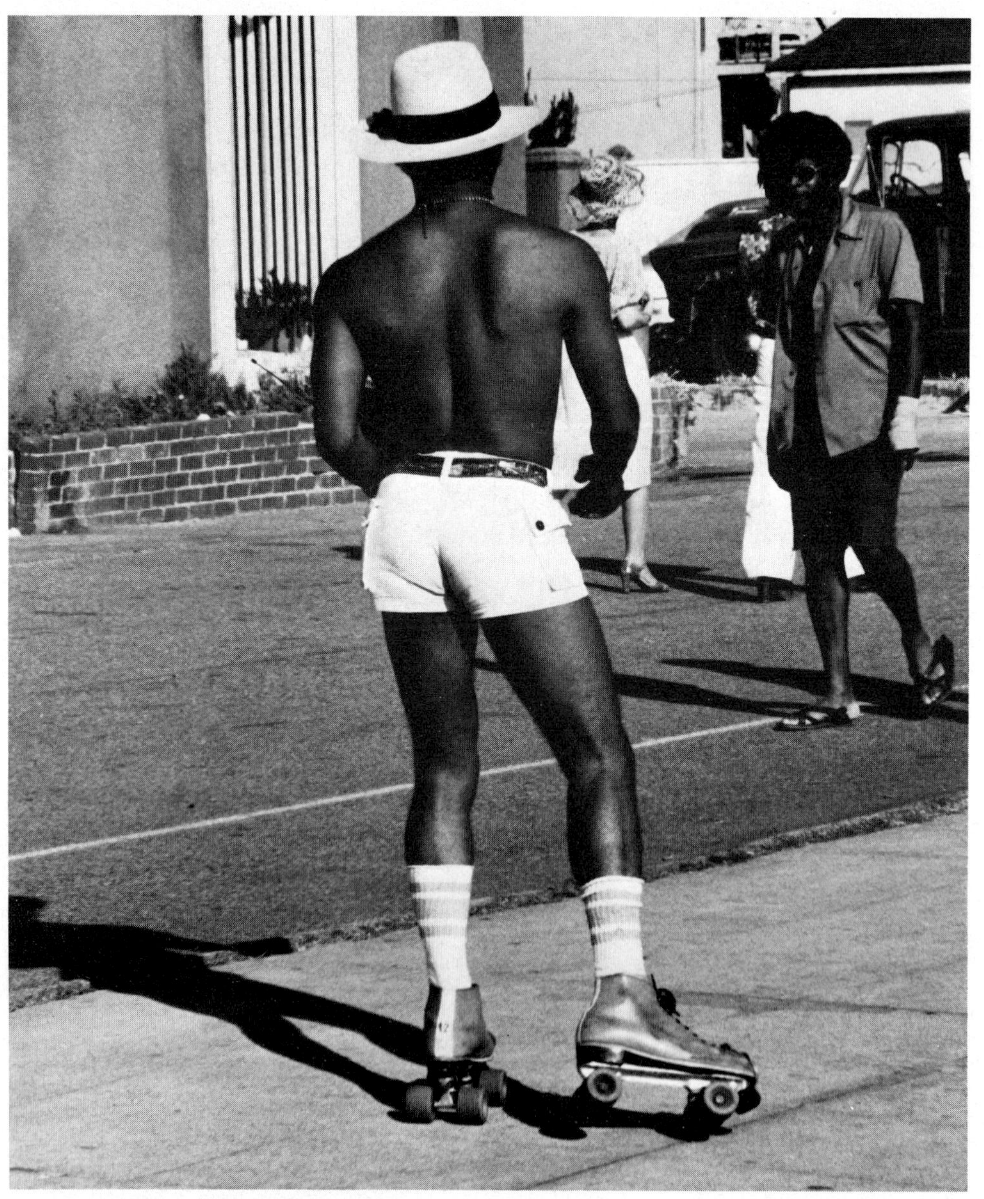

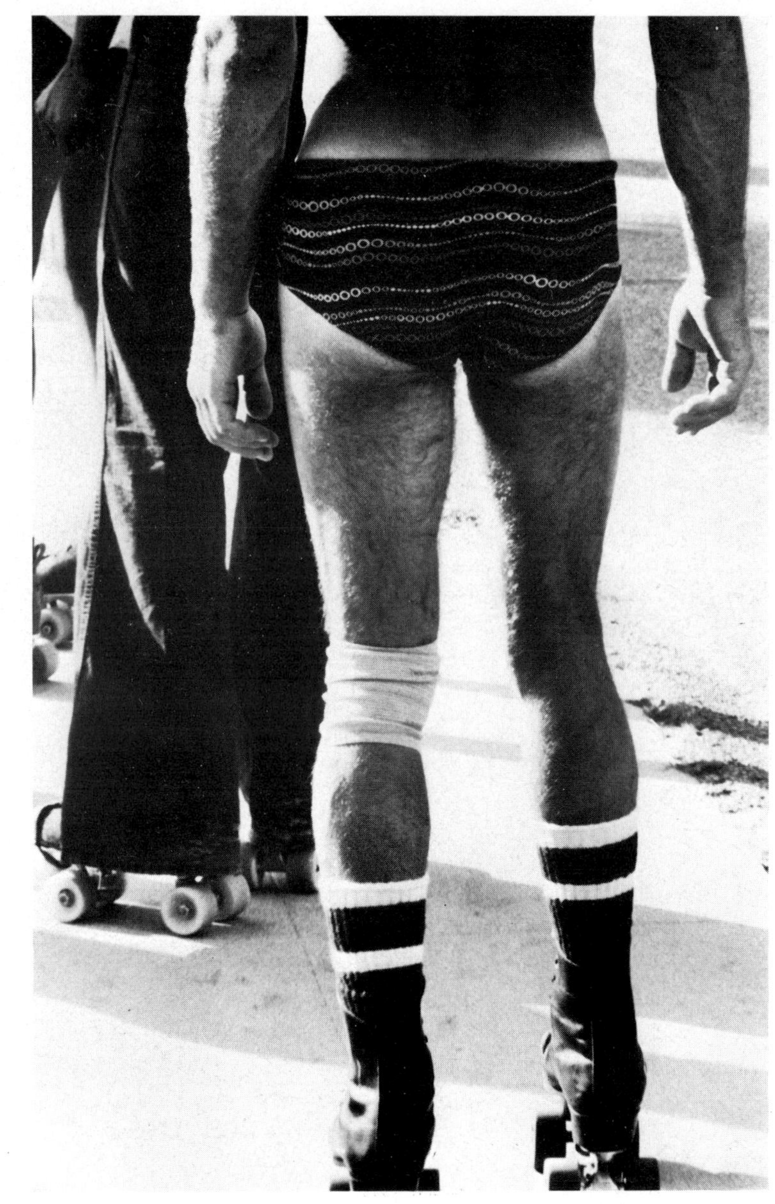

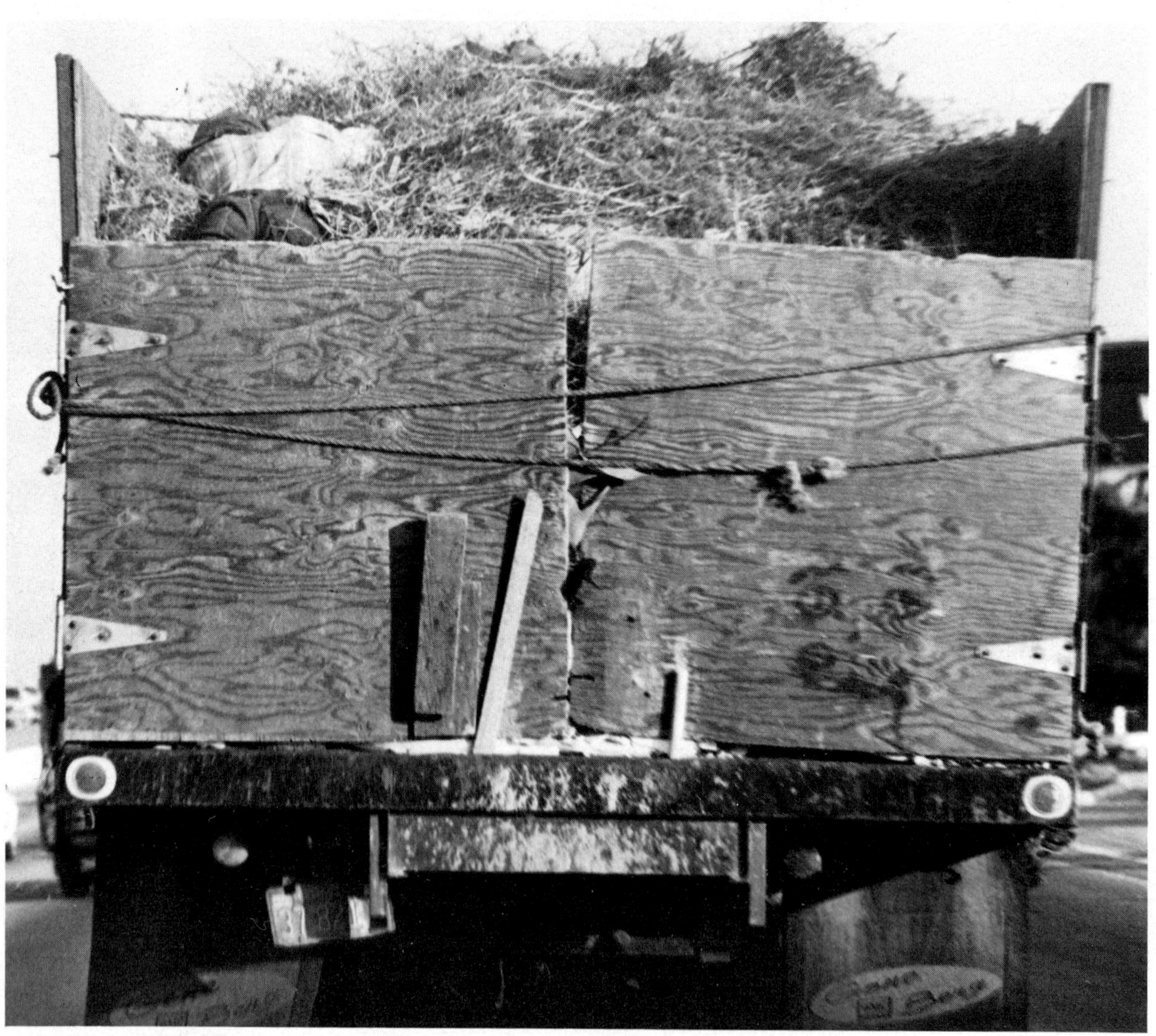

Hauling ass